P9-DXT-244

Schaum's Quick Guide to Writing Great Short Stories

Other Books in Schaum's Quick Guide Series include:

SCHAUM'S QUICK GUIDE TO BUSINESS FORMULAS

SCHAUM'S QUICK GUIDE TO WRITING GREAT ESSAYS

SCHAUM'S QUICK GUIDE TO GREAT PRESENTATION SKILLS

Schaum's Quick Guide to Writing Great Short Stories

Margaret Lucke

McGraw-Hill

New York   San Francisco   Washington, D.C.   Auckland   Bogotá
Caracas   Lisbon   London   Madrid   Mexico City   Milan
Montreal   New Delhi   San Juan   Singapore
Sydney   Tokyo   Toronto

Library of Congress Catalog Card Number: 98-067035 [ED--Insert correct #]

Lucke, Margaret.
   Schaum's quick guide to writing great short stories / Margaret
Lucke.
       p.   cm.
   Includes index.
   ISBN 0-07-039077-0
   1. Short story—Technique.   I. Title.
PN3373.L77   1998
808.3'1—dc21   98-31510
                                                      CIP

McGraw-Hill

A Division of The *McGraw·Hill* Companies

Copyright © 1999 by The McGraw-Hill Companies, Inc. All rights reserved. Printed in
the United States of America. Except as permitted under the United States Copyright
Act of 1976, no part of this publication may be reproduced or distributed in any form
or by any means, or stored in a database or retrieval system, without the prior written
permission of the publisher.

           12 13 14 15 16 DOC/DOC 1 5 4 3 2 1 0

ISBN 0-07-039077-0

*The sponsoring editor for this book was Mary Loebig-Giles, the editing supervisor was Fred
Dahl, the designer was Inkwell Publishing Services, and the production supervisor was
Sherri Souffrance. It was set in Stone Serif by Inkwell Publishing Services.*

Printed and bound by R. R. Donnelley & Sons Company.

McGraw-Hill books are available at special quantity discounts to use as premiums and
sales promotions, or for use in corporate training sessions. For more information,
please write to the Director of Special Sales, McGraw-Hill, Two Penn Plaza, New York,
NY 10121-2298. Or contact your local bookstore.

To Scott,
as he explores the magic of creative expression

Contents

1. Writing a Short Story—Getting Started   1

What Is a Short Story?   2

Finding a Story to Write   5

A Short Story's Basic Ingredients   10

Sitting Down to Write   12

Exercises: Generating Ideas   19

**2. Characters—How to Create People
Who Live and Breathe on the Page**   21

Choosing a Protagonist   22

Choosing a Point of View   23

Bringing Your Characters to Life   29

Tip Sheet: Three-Dimensional Characters   39

Character's Bio Chart   41

Giving Your Characters a Voice   42

Tip Sheet: Dialogue   49

Exercises: Creating Characters   51

**3. Conflict—How to Devise a Story
That Readers Won't Want to Put Down**   55

How Conflict Works in a Short Story   56

The Protagonist's Predicament   57

Bad Guys, Hurricanes, and Fatal Flaws   60

Conflict Equals Suspense   63

Exercises: Finding Story Conflict   66

4. Plot and Structure—How to Shape Your Story and Keep It Moving Forward   69

What Is a Plot?   69

Four Characteristics of a Plot   72

Building the Narrative Structure   79

Beginnings, Middles, and Ends   83

Chart: Narrative Structure   84

Scenes: The Building Blocks of a Plot   92

Stories without Plots   94

Exercises: Constructing a Plot   96

5. Setting and Atmosphere—How to Bring Readers into a Vivid Story World   99

Choosing Your Setting   101

Bringing Your Setting to Life   107

Tip Sheet: Three-Dimensional Settings   115

Exercises: Making a Setting Vivid   118

6. Narrative Voice—How to Develop Your Individual Voice As a Writer   121

What Is Voice?   122

Making Your Voice Stronger   124

Making Your Voice Your Own   132

Tip Sheet: Narrative Voice   134

Exercises: Discovering and Developing Your Voice   138

Appendix A: Suggested Reading—Exploring the Realm of Short Stories   143

Appendix B: When Your Story Is Written—A Quick Guide to Submitting Manuscripts for Publication   147

Appendix C: How to Format Your Manuscript   153

Index   157

Acknowledgments

I would like to express my deep appreciation and gratitude to:

The students in my writing classes, who have challenged and inspired me with their questions, their insights, and their wonderful stories.

My writer colleagues and friends, with whose encouragement I have discovered so much about what I know about writing. To mention only a few: Dave Bischoff, Lawrence Block, Janet Dawson, Susan Dunlap, Syd Field, Suzanne Gold, Jonnie Jacobs, Theo Kuhlmann, Bette Golden Lamb, J.J. Lamb, Janet LaPierre, George Leonard, Lynn MacDonald, Larry Menkin, Marcia Muller, Bill Pronzini, Shelley Singer, Laurel Trivelpiece, Penny Warner, Mary Wings, Judith Yamamoto, and Chelsea Quinn Yarbro. There are many more, and I value them all.

Mary Loebig Giles and Don Gastwirth, who gave me the opportunity to write this book.

Charlie and Agness, who have been supportive, patient, and generous throughout the process, as they always are.

Margaret Lucke

Schaum's Quick Guide to Writing Great Short Stories

Chapter 1

Writing the Short Story

Getting Started

Once upon a time—what a magical phrase. It offers an irresistible invitation: *Settle back and listen. I'm going to tell you a story.*

Few pleasures are as basic and satisfying as hearing a good story—unless it's the pleasure of writing one.

The concept of stories must have been invented as soon as human whoops and squeals turned into language. Stories have been found recorded on papyrus from ancient Egypt and in the fragments of documents that were compiled to become the Judeo-Christian Scriptures. It's possible that the smudgy cave paintings of prehistoric eras were made to illustrate tales told around cooking fires about the trials and tribulations of the season's hunt. Civilizations around the globe have used stories to preserve history, define heroes, and explain the caprices of the gods. The impulse to tell stories is no less strong today.

Writers write for two reasons. One is that they have something they want to say. The other, equally compelling motive is that they have something they want to find out. Writing is a mode of exploration. Through stories we can examine and come to terms with our own ideas, insights, and experiences. In the process of writing a story, we achieve a little better understanding of our world, our fellows, and ourselves. When someone reads what we write, we can share a bit of that understanding.

What's more, writing a story can be great fun.

So sharpen your pencils or fire up your computer, and let's get started.

What Is a Short Story?

We begin with a couple of dictionary definitions. The first defines a story as "the telling of a happening or a series of connected events." Another definition of a short story is "a narrative...designed to interest, amuse, or inform the hearer or reader."

These are the first of many definitions we'll encounter in the course of this book. Each definition has its uses, although none completely captures the essence of what a short story is. When taken together, they will all contribute to your sense of what constitutes a short story and what makes one story satisfying to read while another is less so.

We will concentrate on the traditional story—the kind that derives its power from characters, actions, and plot; that has a beginning, a middle, and an end. Not all short stories are like this. An advantage of the short story form is that its brevity allows variations and experiments that would be difficult to sustain throughout the much longer course of a novel. A short story writer can focus on sketching a character, presenting a slice of life, playing with language, or evoking a mood. Many excellent stories written and published today achieve their impact from the way the author assembles a mosaic of images or jagged fragments of experience, instead of telling an old-fashioned tale. But the traditional story provides the best vantage point for examining the craft of short story writing.

The best way to get a solid feel for the short story as a literary form is to learn from the stories themselves. Become a voracious and eclectic reader. Read stories in abundance. Read literary stories and stories from a variety of genres—mystery, science fiction, fantasy, horror, romance. Read classic stories by acknowledged masters and recently published works by writers whose reputations are still developing. Read traditional stories and experimental ones. You will gain an intuitive sense of how to make a story work.

Then do the three things that are essential to becoming a short story writer:

1. Write.

2. Write some more.

3. Keep on writing.

FICTION VERSUS REALITY

When you write a short story you use the raw material of your imagination, your experience, and your observations about how life works to construct a small but complete and self-contained world. You create a sort of parallel universe that resembles the real world but differs from it in significant ways. Your world may mirror the real one so closely that we as readers accept it as the one we walk around in every day, or it may deviate markedly, especially if you are writing science fiction or fantasy. As the writer, your job is to make your world so vivid and true that readers believe in it, no matter how preposterous it may be when compared to reality.

Two things distinguish a short story world from the actual one: In real life, events occur haphazardly, while in fiction they have a purpose. Because of that, a short story doesn't leave us hanging, perplexed about the outcome, the way life does. We have the satisfaction of achieving resolution and a sense of closure.

THE STORY GOAL

In the two dictionary definitions already cited, the key words are *connected* and *designed*. Unlike your holiday letter to Aunt Sue, in a short story the events described are not random. The author chooses, organizes, and describes them with a design or purpose in mind. What connects the events is the contribution each one makes to the accomplishment of this unifying goal.

There are many possible story goals. You might wish to examine some aspect of human nature, or to help yourself and your readers understand what it's like to go through some experience. You could be striving to create a particular mood or evoke a certain emotion within your readers: *This story's going to scare the bejeebers out of them.*

Whatever your goal might be, it becomes the organizing principle of the story, giving it cohesion, coherence, and a sense of completeness. The decisions you make about the story—who the characters are, what incidents are depicted, where the incidents take place, how the story is structured, what words are chosen to tell it—all derive from the goal. Anything extraneous, however brilliant or profound it may be, can distract both you and your reader from the purpose of the story.

Does having a goal sound lofty and a bit daunting? Don't worry, you don't have to climb Mount Everest. Scaling a gentle slope will do just as well. "A narrative...designed to interest, amuse, or inform the reader"—there are infinite ways, large and small, to interest, amuse, and inform.

Nor do you need to have clearly identified your goal before you start. As we noted, writing a short story is a process of exploration—a search not only to find answers, but often to figure out what the questions are. As you plan your story and write the early drafts, you'll gain a clearer focus on the goal you want to pursue.

RESOLUTION OR CLOSURE

The advantage of having a story goal is that it gives you a direction to head in and a destination to reach. When you arrive you're rewarded with a sense of resolution or closure that's rare in real life. Both writer and reader get to find out how it all comes out.

This means that the major questions posed by the story get answered before the words *The End* appear. It doesn't mean that there can be no ambiguities left, or that the reader will know for sure that the characters will (or won't) live happily ever after. But the story achieves its own kind of completeness: These connected events have reached their logical conclusion. Anything else that might happen belongs in a new story.

A WORD ABOUT THEME

Someone may ask you, "What is the theme of your story?" and chances are you won't know what to say.

"Come on," this person will persist, "every story has to have a theme."

Well, perhaps. It's true that in many effective stories the small, specific details of the characters, the setting, and the events that take place serve to illustrate some abstract concept or larger idea—the nature of justice, say, or the consequences of exploiting the environment, or the difference between romantic and parental love.

Sometimes the desire to explore a certain theme provides your initial idea, your story goal. But it may be that you will complete several drafts before you realize what the theme is. In fact, you can write a story that a reader will find compelling, insightful, and moving without being consciously aware of its theme at all. The theme emerges quietly as you pay attention to all the other details of your writing art and craft.

HOW LONG IS SHORT?

Ideally, a short story should be exactly as long as it needs to be, and no longer or shorter. In other words, use the number of words you need to tell the story in the most effective way.

Still, there are conventions. Once you get past 20,000 words or so, you are edging past the boundary of the short story into the realm of the novelette. Most magazines and anthologies prefer stories that have 5,000 words or fewer. Some publishers request short-short stories; what they mean by this term varies, but it tends to refer to narratives of no longer than 2,000 words.

In novels, word counts of 75,000 to 100,000 are typical and greater lengths are not uncommon; you have latitude to ramble, to take side roads and detours, to reminisce or digress or offer philosophical observations. You can span decades, even epochs as James Michener did in novels like *Chesapeake* and *Hawaii*. You can roam worldwide.

But precisely because they are short, short stories require a tighter focus. The illumination they offer is less like an overhead light and more like a flashlight's beam. Rather than recount its main character's life history, the short story usually concentrates on a single relationship, a significant incident, or a defining moment.

Finding a Story to Write

To begin writing a story you need an idea. That simple requirement stops many aspiring writers before they start.

Where do you get your ideas? This question has a reputation for being the one writers are most often asked, and the one some of them are most tired of hearing. I heard one writer huff: "It's as if people expect me to name a catalog where they can order up ideas—guaranteed to generate a good story or your money back."

But the question is worth pondering, all the more so because there are no pat answers. The idea is the spark that ignites the creative process, one of the most mysterious and fascinating of human endeavors.

Experienced writers have ideas all the time, which is why they may find the question perplexing and occasionally tedious. Coming up with ideas is easy; the problem is finding time to sit down and write.

The fact is, ideas are everywhere. The trick is to recognize them and grab them as they go by.

AN IDEA IS TO A WRITER...

The problem, I think, is that people misunderstand the relationship between an idea and a story. An idea is anything that kick-starts your imagination with enough power to begin the story creation process. It's whatever catches hold of your mind long enough for you to think: "Hmmm. I wonder if there's a story in there someplace."

That's all a story idea is. One thing that blocks would-be writers is that they expect their initial idea to be larger than that, to give them more of the answers than it will. They believe the following analogy to be true:

An idea is to a writer as a seed is to a gardener.

In other words, they think that once a writer finds an idea, the story inevitably follows. The gardening analogy suggests that the idea, like a seed, holds a genetic blueprint for the story that predetermines the nature of its characters, plot, and setting, in the same way that a bulb contains the tulip or an acorn contains the future oak tree. Stick the idea in soil, sprinkle on a little water, and the story will spring up and blossom almost of its own accord.

That's a misperception. Here's a closer analogy:

An idea is to a writer as flour is to a baker.

A story idea really functions more like the flour you use to make bread or pastry. It is the first ingredient, and an essential one. But you need to choose various other ingredients, blend them in, and bake them all together before you have a treat that's ready to serve.

A story is an aggregation of many ideas, large and small. Each idea contributes to and yet changes the final result, like ingredients combined in a recipe. As with baking, when you write a story a sort of chemical reaction takes place. The final product is something more than the sum of its ingredients. It becomes something entirely new, and the individual ingredients can no longer be separated out.

Your initial inspiration can lead you to any number of stories. What you add to the flour idea determines whether you end up creating chocolate cake or apple pie, sugar cookies or sourdough rolls.

SOURCES OF IDEAS

The flour idea for your story can be anything—a character, a situation or incident, an intriguing place, a theme you want to explore. When you're lucky, story ideas just pop into your head. These are little gifts from your subconscious, and we all have more of them than we realize. Usually they come while we are thinking about something else entirely or about nothing at all. For me they are often associated with water—ideas float into my mind when I'm swimming or taking a shower. It's a little game my subconscious mind plays with me, giving me ideas when I have no paper and pencil handy to write them down.

The flour idea for my short story *Identity Crisis* was this kind of brainflash: a single line of dialogue. In my mind's ear I heard a young woman ask another: "Do I look like a corpse to you?" All I had to do was figure out who the women were, what prompted the question, and what they were going to do about the answer. Writer Chris Rogers was nodding off to sleep one night when a dreamlike image drifted by: a shiny Jaguar in a used car lot filled with old junkers. What's that doing there, she wondered, and the story creation process began.

But you don't have to wait for your subconscious mind to feel generous. Conduct an active search for ideas—your everyday life is full of them. You can find them in the people you encounter, the places you go, the events you take part in or witness, the things that you read. A story might be sparked by the argument you have with a coworker, the memory of that embarrassing moment at your senior prom, your mother's recollection of her eccentric Uncle Harry, a snatch of conversation you overhear from the next booth in the coffee shop, a magazine article that makes you wonder, "Why would people behave like that?"

We are not all writers, but most of us are storytellers. We relate stories constantly: the funny thing that happened at school today, the time when we went camping and got lost in the mountains. Listen to the incidents you hear yourself describing over and over, the episodes that have become part of your history, the ones that leave your friends rolling their eyes and saying, "Oh no, not this story again." If a tale engages you so much that you repeat it to all your new acquaintances, then there might well be a good short story there.

SYNERGY: IDEAS IN TEAMWORK

The truth is, one idea is seldom enough.

Suppose you have come up with a wonderful idea on which to base a story, one that keeps nudging at your brain, demanding to be written. But all you have is a fragment—an image of an old woman riding a train, an offhand comment made by a friend, a glimpse of an old house that surely must be haunted. The flour just sits there in the bowl, waiting for you to decide on the next ingredient.

When you figure out what you want to add to the flour, that's when the story begins to come alive. The story develops from the synergy that occurs when two ideas mesh.

Karen Cushman, author of the *The Ballad of Lucy Whipple*, has said that the idea for that story came to her in a museum bookstore in California's gold country. Reading about the gold rush, she was struck by the statistic that ninety percent of the people who flooded into California in the early 1850s were men. That meant that ten percent were women and children, but one rarely heard about them. What would life have been like for a girl, she wondered, in such a rough, raw territory? Cushman herself had endured an unwelcome cross-country move as a child. So now she had two elements to work with: the notion of a child's perspective on an exciting moment in history, coupled with her own experience and feelings as a twelve-year-old uprooted from a familiar and comfortable home. When these ideas teamed up, the character of Lucy Whipple was born.

Margaret Atwood commented in a radio interview that she thinks a lot of stories begin as questions. One that she asked herself was: "If you were going to take over the United States, how would you do it?" Another was: "If women's place isn't in the home, how are you going to get them to go back there when they don't want to go?" Either question by itself had the potential to lead to an intriguing story. But it was when Atwood combined the two that the story process began in earnest, resulting in her novel, *The Handmaid's Tale*.

THINKING STORY: THE "WHAT IF..." GAME

Writers train themselves to "think story"—to look at people, places, and situations with an eye to discerning what dramatic potential they might contain.

Your subconscious constantly gives you clues about where to begin. Whenever something jiggles your mind enough to make you think, "That's interesting..." or, "I wonder...," it's a signal that a story idea is there, waiting for you to discover it.

The next step is to think, "What if..." Make it a game to discover the story possibilities around you.

Suppose you're lunching at a cafe, and you notice a young woman with a green silk scarf sitting at the window table. She's been there for an hour, nursing a cappuccino and impatiently looking at her watch. What's going on?

What if she's waiting for her lover? What if she has sneaked away from her job to grab a few minutes with him, risking her boss's anger? What if she is married, meeting her lover in secret, and her mother strolls by and sees her in the cafe window? Or her husband does? What if her lover then shows up? Or what if he never shows up and she decides to find out why?

Another scenario: What if the young woman has discovered that the company she works for is defrauding its clients? What if she has arranged to meet a police detective who is investigating similar frauds? What if the green scarf is a signal so that the detective will recognize her, and the briefcase by her chair is filled with incriminating documents?

You can play the "what if..." game anywhere. At the airport, as you wait for your delayed plane to board, pick one or two of your fellow passengers—the man in the business suit slumped in the hard seat, perhaps, or the redheaded girl sipping coffee from a paper cup. Think story: Why are they making this trip? What awaits them at their final destination? How will their lives be made difficult by this flight's being late?

In line at the supermarket, contemplate the young woman behind you with the squalling infant in her cart. Where does she live, and who is waiting for her there? What if she walks into her apartment and finds her husband at home when he should be at work? Or what if she's expecting her husband to greet her, but when she arrives he is gone? What if she then finds a cryptic note on the kitchen table?

A volume of excellent story ideas can be delivered to your doorstep every day: the newspaper. Pick an article that intrigues you and try the "what if..." game. The point is not to make a story out of the actual circumstances that are described or to turn the real people involved into fictional characters. What you want to do is isolate the basic situation and draw a brand new story out of it. You might try working from the headline alone.

For instance, suppose the headline reads: "Government Official Is Arrested by USA on Espionage Charges." Ignore the article and let your imagination play. Who is this person, and what led him or her to become a spy? What if he's been falsely accused and is not guilty? What if it's a case of mistaken identity? What if his boss set him up to take the fall? What if he is in fact a double agent, pretending to spy for a foreign government but really gathering information for the CIA?

To get your imagination really humming, try to come up with three or more scenarios for each person, place, or situation that triggers a "what if...."

A Short Story's Basic Ingredients

Now that you have an idea for a story, let's revisit our second dictionary definition and expand on that word *designed* a bit. Our revised definition is this: A short story is "a short narrative in which the author combines elements of character, conflict, plot, and setting in an artful way to interest, amuse, or inform the reader."

The four elements and the artful way in which the author presents them are the essential ingredients of any short story—the sugar, eggs, cinnamon, and cream that you knead together to turn your story idea into a bread or pastry that is tasty and satisfying.

In the following chapters, we'll take an in-depth look at these five topics—the basic crafts of short story writing. We'll examine the contribution each of the ingredients makes to the story and how they interact, influencing its development.

- **Characters.** No matter how compelling your initial idea is, it won't come alive until you conjure up some imaginary people and hand it to them. Through their motivations, actions, and responses, they create the story. For a truly satisfying story, skip ordering up stock figures from central casting and breathe life into your characters, making them as solid and complex and real as you and your readers are. Chapter Two shows you how.

- **Conflict.** This is the life's blood of your story, flowing through it and giving it energy. The conflict you set up propels the events of the story and raises the issues that must be resolved. In taking action to deal with it, your characters reveal themselves: their motivations, weaknesses, and strengths. Chapter Three examines how conflict drives the story and creates the suspense that keeps readers hooked until the last page.

- **Plot and structure.** The structure of a story is like the framing of a house or the skeleton inside a body: It organizes and gives shape to the disparate parts. Once you know who your characters are and what conflict they face, you can explore how you want to arrange and present the story's events, from beginning to middle to end. Although there are other ways to structure a story, Chapter Four concentrates on the traditional method which, though it was first explored in ancient times, still offers tremendous challenges and satisfactions to writers and readers alike—the construction of an effective plot.

■ **Setting and atmosphere.** A story's setting provides a context for its characters and events. Not only does it situate them in time and place, but it shapes the people and influences what happens to them. It influences readers too. When your setting is vivid and your atmosphere supports the story's tone and mood, you bring readers right inside the story, increasing their involvement in what's going on. Chapter Five explains how to create this you-are-there effect.

■ **Narrative voice.** The first four elements constitute the who, why, what, when, and where of the story; they define what the story is about. The fifth element is the how, the "artful way" the story is told.

The term *voice* encompasses all the choices a writer makes about language and style. It also includes the unique perspective that any author brings to his or her own work. Had Ernest Hemingway and William Faulkner ever described the same set of events, the resulting stories would have been very different, thanks to their strong and distinctive voices.

Beginner or pro, every writer has a voice, whether conscious of it or not. Novice writers often borrow someone else's voice, and it may fit the writer no better than a suit of borrowed clothes would. One mark of a writer's growing skill is the increased willingness to "say it my way" and to do so with care and precision. Chapter Six will help you to understand the concept of voice, and to discover and develop your own.

Sitting Down to Write

Okay, you have some ideas for your story and a few thoughts about how to put them together. Now comes the tricky part: Writing the darn thing. Here are four important things to remember as you sit down, pen in hand or fingers on the keyboard.

I. THERE ARE NO RULES.

Author W. Somerset Maugham once said: "There are three rules for writing a novel. Unfortunately, no one knows what they are." This wise comment applies equally to short stories.

What you read in this book (or anywhere else) are suggestions, observations, things that might offer some insight, points that it might be helpful to keep in mind. As you read, you are sure to encounter plenty of stories, some of them excellent, that defy or contradict every key point that I make. Part of growing as a writer is honing your own instinct for what does and does not work in a story and developing confidence in your own choices.

Writing a story is a nonlinear process. You can't go from Step One, to Step Two, to Step Three, from beginning to end, the way you would assemble a bookcase or even (despite our earlier analogy) the way you would bake a cake. You move forward, then backward. Inward, then outward. Down side roads and around in circles. Eventually, if you stick with it, you have finished writing a story.

A story begins with a single idea, a glimmering—something that niggles at your brain and says, "Follow me." So that's what you do. There's no predicting where it will lead you. Many a writer, upon finishing a manuscript, realizes that the finished product bears little resemblance to the story she thought she was setting out to write. As you begin the first draft, you may have only the faintest notion of what the final story will be. Even when you decide on an ending early on, you can't know how you or your characters will get there until you actually undertake the journey, and you may discover that your destination changes as you travel along.

A story evolves. Writing one is like holding a conversation between your conscious and subconscious minds. The process is fraught with contradictions. A story must be focused and organized, yet the creation of it, especially in the early stages, tends to be unfocused and disorganized. The author must keep control of the story and at the same time let go of it, allowing the elements of characters, conflict, structure, setting, and voice to push on each other, to interact and mix and mingle and romp in rough-and-tumble fashion until the story is done.

There are no absolutes in writing fiction, no right way or wrong way to do it. The right way for you is the way that lets you achieve your own goal for the story most effectively. Your success is measured only in terms of how well the story satisfies you and your readers.

2. THERE IS NO MAGIC FORMULA.

An editor with a New York publishing firm—I'll call him John Samuels—once told me about an experience he had when he was speaking at a writers conference. His topic was, "What Editors Look for in a Manuscript." The room was packed with aspiring writers eager to achieve publication. They were bright-eyed and excited. Their notebooks were open and ready. Yet as he spoke, addressing some of the same subjects we'll be talking about in this book—creating strong characters, devising a compelling plot—John realized he was losing his audience. Their minds were wandering, their heads nodding. From the back of the room, he thought he heard someone snore.

Then, about halfway through the hour, a woman raised her hand. "Mr. Samuels," she said, "you're not sticking to the topic. You're supposed to tell us what editors want. So let's talk about that. Now, when I send in my manuscript, how wide should I make the margins?"

John wasn't surprised at the question. He hears at least one off-the-wall question every time he gives a talk. What surprised and dismayed him was that suddenly the whole audience became alert, sat up straight in their chairs, and poised their pens over their notebooks, ready to take down John's magic formula for writing success. Make the margins precisely this wide, and you will be published.

If only it were that easy. Of course margins count, because a properly prepared manuscript demonstrates to an editor that you have a professional attitude, that you know what you're doing. If you present your story in its correct business attire, the editor will read it with a higher expectation that it will be publishable; if your manuscript looks sloppy or careless, the editor may not read your story at all. But plenty of neatly typed manuscripts with one-inch margins all around are rejected. What matters to both editors and readers are the art and the craft you bring to the writing of the story itself.

Achieving art and craft in short story writing requires hard work and dedication. In the process, you will become frustrated and dejected, you will wad up pages of leaden prose and false starts and dead ends and fling them across the room. You will be tempted to smash your computer screen or heave your typewriter out the window.

But what is far more important, you will also experience great joy. You will have moments when you become so absorbed in the fictional world you are creating that time will seem to stop; days when you sit down at your desk after breakfast and look up just minutes later to realize that it's dinnertime. You will experience the high that comes after one of those rare days when when prose flows, the characters don't balk, and the story takes on a life of its own. You will know the exhilaration of hearing someone who has no vested interest in saying so tell you, "Hey, I read your story. It's really good."

Some writers maintain that writing can't be taught. Perhaps this is true, especially when it comes to the art of the writing, because the art is born of the individual vision and insights and passions that the writer brings to the work.

But the craft of writing, if it can't be taught, can certainly be learned. Learning is a process of trial and error. Take classes, listen to writers speak, read this book and others, do the exercises that they suggest. Try the suggested tips and techniques in your own writing, and see which ones work for you.

What you will discover is that there is no foolproof recipe for writing a short story. There is no definitive set of instructions. There is no secret that, if only you can persuade someone to whisper it in your ear, will guarantee success.

For every writer, the creative process works differently. Every writer uses different techniques for tapping into her creativity, keeping track of her ideas, and managing her writing activities. There are writers who work best in the early morning, and others who can't get juiced up until the late news signs off. In this age of technological sophistication, I know one author who, after eighteen published books, still pecks out her stories with two fingers on an old typewriter. I know another who writes all his first drafts in longhand on yellow legal pads. All of these writers are doing it right—for them.

3. YOU DON'T HAVE TO GET IT RIGHT THE FIRST TIME.

As you sit down to begin a new story, you're likely to feel unsure of yourself. There is so much about these characters and this situation that you don't yet know. Even if you did know all about them, how can you get it all down on paper so that it reads well?

Not to worry: You don't have to get it right the first time. You can take advantage of a wonderful invention called the second draft.

One thing that intimidates new writers is the infernal internal editor—that dastardly creature that sits on your shoulder and keeps up a constant nattering: "That's atrocious. You spelled that word wrong. Why did you say it that way? You don't know enough to write about that. Everything you're writing is mush."

Hard as it may be, refuse to listen to this little monster, especially while you're writing the first draft. Later on your internal editor can be your friend, provided you keep it on a strong leash. But while the first draft is under way it is your enemy. It derives its greatest satisfaction from preventing you from writing your story.

The trick is to ignore its nagging and whining and plunge on. Give yourself permission to be a terrible writer until you've completed the entire first draft. If you surrender to the beastie's urgings and keep rewriting page one until it's perfect, you'll end up with a fat drawerful of beautiful page ones, but very few stories.

I recommend writing at least three drafts of your story, each draft being a version of the whole story, from beginning to end:

- **Draft one: What to say.** The purpose of the first draft is to let you discover the story. As you write it, you become acquainted with the characters, sort out the events, figure out what is meaningful and what is not. Just let the story pour out. Don't worry about spelling or punctuation or pretty phrasing or whether you've got something right. Sure, the quality of the writing will be embarrassing and awful, but that's fine. No one but you will ever see it. As you go along you may realize that you need to hint that Aunt Clara is afraid of heights back when you introduce her on page two, in order to lay the groundwork for the scene on the cliff that begins on page twelve. Fine. Jot a reminder to yourself on page two and deal with it when you rewrite.

- **Draft two: How to say it.** This is when your internal editor can turn from foe to friend, from demon to angel—as long as you keep straight in your mind that you're the one in charge. Your editor can give you the judgment to figure out what works in the story and what needs attention, to discover a better way to describe a character or express an idea. Now is the time to insert a mention of Aunt Clara's acrophobia, to decide that Dave and Lynne's argument should take place in the kitchen instead of the cocktail lounge, to take out the wonderful scene with the yellow cat because, even though it's the best thing you've ever written, a cat doesn't belong in this story. In this draft you smooth out clunky language, adjust the pace of the scenes, and make sure you have achieved your intended mood, rhythm, and tone. Here you make sure the loose ends are tied up and that each element—character, conflict, plot, setting, and voice—contributes to the cohesiveness of the story as a whole.

■ **Draft three: Cut and polish.** In this go-round, you make sure that every word pulls its weight, that any flab is trimmed out, that your prose flows smoothly, that your spelling and grammar are impeccable.

Three is not a magic number. Each "draft" might be a series of drafts, entailing more than one trip through the manuscript. You could rework a certain scene several times before it's the way you want it to be. I once read that Ernest Hemingway rewrote the last chapter of *A Farewell to Arms* 119 times, although I can't imagine that he actually kept count.

Remember, though, that no story will ever be perfect. There is a time to declare the story finished and let it go. Ignore that little voice that keeps telling you, "It's not good enough yet. It still has flaws. Someone might criticize it. Don't let anyone see it. Work on it some more." It's your infernal internal editor again, back in enemy mode and trying to thwart you. Don't let it win.

4. IF YOU DON'T WRITE YOUR STORY, IT WON'T GET WRITTEN.

Writing a story is not a task you can delegate. In the process of creating a story, you bring your own insights, experiences, and imagination to bear. Whatever the genre, whatever the subject matter, no one else could possibly write the same story that you would write. If you don't write it, no one will ever have the pleasure of reading it or the benefit of sharing your vision.

There is a saying among writers: "I don't want to write; I want to have written." Wouldn't it be wonderful if the rewards of writing could be ours without all the nasty hard work that goes into earning them?

Unfortunately, you can't reach that second place without going through the first. You never will have written unless at some point you actually sit down and write.

A common error would-be writers make is to hang back and wait for inspiration to strike. But writing is nine-tenths perspiration. The writer and teacher Larry Menkin always said the most important advice on writing he could offer his students was this: "Apply seat of pants." Apply the seat of your own pants to the chair in front of your computer or desk, and start writing.

The fact is, inspiration is most likely to tap you on the shoulder when you are actively involved in the writing process. Like many writers, you'll probably find that when you're working on a story, fresh ideas for that story and new ones will bubble up most readily.

So, as we move on to look at the basic ingredients of fiction, remember the three things you should do if you want to be a writer of short stories:

1. Write.
2. Write some more.
3. Keep on writing.

Exercises: Generating Ideas

1. Open a book, copy out a single sentence at random, and close the book. Without referring to its context in the original work, begin with that sentence and keep writing. Let the words flow; don't stop or put down your pen. Try this three times, taking off from the sentence in a new direction each time.

2. Pick a photo in a magazine or newspaper. A photo with two or more people in it will work best. What led these people to this moment? What happens next? Come up with three possibilities for before and after. Select one and write a scene describing it.

3. Choose three articles from today's newspaper. For each one, write a single sentence describing the basic situation. Without referring to the real people or circumstances involved, play the "what if..." game to develop the situation into a story. Write a scene that could belong in each of the three stories you come up with.

4. As you go through your day's activities (on the bus, in a restaurant, at the library), notice an interesting-looking stranger whom you are unlikely to see again. Playing "what if...," and without speaking to the person, guess why he or she is there, where he came from, where he is going next and who else is involved. Come up with three possibilities, and write a scene from each story.

5. Ask yourself the following questions and write down the first answer that comes to mind:

   a. What is the most **exciting** thing you can think of? What is something that, if it happened to you, would be just incredibly thrilling, or wonderful, or fun?

   b. What is the most **dangerous** thing you've ever been seriously tempted to do?

   c. What is the most **embarrassing** or **humiliating** situation you've ever been in?

   d. What is something that makes you really **angry**? What really makes your blood boil?

e. What is the most **frightening** thing you can think of? What, if it happened to you, would have the most devastating effect on your life?

Pick one answer, and write a scene using that situation as its basis. However, don't place yourself or real people you know in the scene; create new characters for the events to happen to. Use the "what if..." game for help.

6. Write about what would have happened if your favorite childhood dream had come true. Think of three positive things that might have resulted. Then think of three negative things. Choose one of these possibilities and write a scene describing it.

Chapter 2

Characters

How to Create People
Who Live and Breathe on the Page

Now that you have an idea for a story, you need to give it away.

What's that? you say. But it's *my* idea. Why should I give it away?

Because it doesn't belong to you, that's why. It belongs to your characters.

Characters are the first essential ingredient in any successful story. Your idea won't come alive, won't begin to become a story, until some characters claim it as their own. The story comes out of their motives, their desires, their actions and interactions and reactions.

It has been said that writing a story is just a matter of dropping some characters into a situation and watching what they do. That's far too simplistic, of course, but the characters are the key to the story. They are ones who must engage readers' attention and sympathy. As we identify with them and become concerned about them, our uncertainty about their fates creates the tension and suspense that keeps us turning the pages.

In a story built around a highly intricate plot, it might seem as though the structure would be the dominant element. But the characters are still paramount. You can't rely on cardboard cutouts to make the machinations of the plot convincing. You need characters in your story who are not only well-rounded and believable, but who suit this particular set of events.

As the author, you expect to be the boss, to have these people firmly under your control. But the best fictional characters have minds of their own. Match the right characters with the right story and they will become valuable collaborators in your creative process.

Choosing a Protagonist

Whose story is this? Who will be your protagonist? This is one of the first decisions you must make.

The protagonist is the hero or heroine of your story. He or she is the central character, the person around whom the events of the story revolve and usually the one who will be most affected by the outcome.

The protagonist is the person with whom readers most closely identify, with whom we form the strongest bond. You want readers to care about him or root for her to succeed. This doesn't mean that your main character has to be thoroughly likable. We readers have faults of our own, and we can empathize with characters who are less than one hundred percent admirable. In John Cheever's story *The Five-Forty-Eight*, we follow a man named Blake as he makes an uneasy commute home from work, stalked the whole way by a young woman who, he fears, intends to do him harm. In the course of the story we come to realize that Blake is self-centered and ruthless, and that the woman may be justified in her anger. Yet Cheever sustains our willingness to identify with Blake until we reach the resolution on the last page.

Make sure your protagonist has a strong personal stake in the matter at hand. Perhaps she has a need to fill or a goal that she must achieve, or she or someone close to her is at risk. When you put a believable character into a compelling situation, the reader will gladly come along for the ride. Sometimes, though, we encounter a lead character who is wandering around to no apparent purpose, while all of the excitement is happening to someone else. If the protagonist doesn't have a good reason to be involved, the reader doesn't either and will likely put the story down unfinished.

Whose story it is affects *what* the story is. Change the protagonist, and the focus of the story must also change. Events affect different people in different ways. If we look at the events through another character's eyes, we will interpret them differently. We'll place our sympathies with someone new. When the conflict arises that is the heart of the story, we will be rooting for a different outcome.

Consider, for example, how the tale of Cinderella would shift if told from the viewpoint of an evil stepsister, as Chelsea Quinn Yarbro did in her short story, *Variations on a Theme*. Or suppose we heard about Romeo and Juliet's romance from the perspective of Juliet's mother. *Gone with the Wind* is Scarlett O'Hara's story, but what if we were shown the same events from the viewpoint of Rhett Butler or Melanie Wilkes?

Who the protagonist should be is not always obvious. Don't automatically give the story to the character who shows up first in your mind or the one who clamors the loudest for your attention. You might have to have two or three characters try on your story idea and model it for you before you discover which one it fits most comfortably.

Let's go back to our newly caught spy from Chapter One. At first glance, the logical protagonist would seem to be the accused man. His story might be fascinating, but it is not the only one you could tell. What is his wife's story? Or his twelve-year-old son's? How about his boss, or his foreign contact, or the young assistant who idolized him? All of these people's lives will be affected by this turn of events, and one of them might offer you a fresher, more intriguing perspective to explore.

If you're writing a story and start feeling stuck, try handing your idea to a new character and letting him run with it. As he carries it off in a new direction, you may be surprised and delighted at the way the story begins to flow again.

Choosing a Point of View

In fiction, point of view refers to the vantage point from which readers observe the events of the story. In other words, whose eyes will we be looking through as we read? As the author, the choice is up to you.

The ways you can handle point of view fall into two major categories, first person and third person. Each has its benefits and disadvantages.

FIRST PERSON

In the first person point of view, one character acts as the narrator, directly telling us her own version of the events. The narrator refers to herself as *I* or *me*, just as you do when you tell a friend what happened to you this afternoon. Here's an example from my short story, *Dreaming of Dragons*:

> I walked north on Grant into a bitter wind, jostling around the horde of pedestrians, the postcard racks, the tables covered with souvenir t-shirts and cloisonné trinkets. The rainy afternoon was brightened by red-and-gold banners fluttering from lampposts, wishing everyone GUNG HAY FAT CHOY—Happy and Prosperous New Year.
>
> When I reached Ming's House of Treasures I was welcomed by a smiling wooden Buddha, four feet high, that stood by the door. A sign was posted beside him: RUB MY HEAD FOR WISDOM OR MY BELLY FOR LUCK. His belly, I noticed, was much shinier than his head.
>
> I massaged Buddha's brow. Better to be wise than lucky, I decided. I felt wiser just from having reached that sensible conclusion.
>
> But inside the shop I had second thoughts. I stepped back out and rubbed the fat tummy, just to be on the safe side.

Most of the time the first person character is the protagonist, but it can be anyone—another major character, a lesser participant, or someone who is simply an observer of the events. In Sir Arthur Conan Doyle's Sherlock Holmes stories, for example, the great detective is the protagonist, but the narrator is his associate, Dr. Watson. The narrator in Ring Lardner's *Haircut* is the town barber, gossiping to a stranger in town about the local citizens. In *A Rose for Emily*, William Faulkner describes a reclusive woman's relationship with her community; the narrator is an unidentified *we* who comes to sound like the voice of the town itself.

First person offers the advantage of strong reader identification with the character. The reader is given an experience that is as direct, intense, and immediate as the character's own, presented in the narrator's natural voice. Because we are in this person's head and heart, we can hear her thoughts and feel her emotions. We get to know her more intimately, and therefore care about her more intensely.

The drawback is that you can tell the reader only what the narrator actually observes or knows firsthand. The narrator cannot climb inside another character's head; she can only guess at his thoughts and feelings based on the evidence of what he says and does. Nor can she know what is happening in a place where she is not present, unless someone tells her about it later.

THIRD PERSON

When you write in the third person, the author, rather than a character, takes on the narrator's role. There is no *I* or *me* in third person, except in dialogue. All of the characters, including the protagonist, are *he, she,* and *they,* as in this example from my story, *No Wildflowers*:

> That spring there were no wildflowers and the grass did not turn green. Every day Sarah scanned the huge blue Oklahoma sky for signs of rain. Occasionally a small white cloud, like a bit of dandelion fluff, would blow by, but nothing more.
>
> Sarah dreamed of home in Virginia, where weeping willows on the creek banks greeted the season with their pale green. Next the world would turn yellow with daffodils and forsythia, then pink and white with azaleas and apple blossoms.
>
> Each morning, while Sarah was dreaming, her husband Rob drove off to the Army post. He was a first lieutenant, paying back the military for putting him through college, and he had two more long, bleak years to go. Sarah attempted to amuse herself until he returned at dinnertime by reading big stacks of romances from the post library, or trying chocolate soufflé recipes she clipped from magazines, or nursing the wilting pansies in the garden she'd scratched into the front lawn of the rented house. For company she had Velvet the cat.
>
> Her violin stayed in its case in the closet, neglected and silent. Sarah tried to ignore the vague sense of guilt that welled up when she thought about practicing and decided, as she always did, *Not today.*

A third person narrative gives you a larger playing field. You can operate on a grander scale, with greater flexibility. You can be in two places at once. You can take your reader inside the minds of more than one character, presenting each person's unique perspective on the story's issues and events. The trade-off is that you sometimes sacrifice the high level of intimacy and the ease of reader identification that a first person narrative affords.

Although there are many subtle variations to the third person point of view, it offers a writer three main options:

- **Limited or restricted third person.** This is similar to first person in that there is one specific viewpoint character. We see the action through his eyes and are privy to his thoughts, and no one else's.

- **Multiple points of view.** In a multiple viewpoint story, we take turns looking through the eyes of two or more viewpoint characters. In this way we gain a more complete understanding of the characters and also of the story's events and issues.

  The usual way to handle multiple viewpoints is to assign each character certain scenes. When you have decided to which character a scene belongs, make sure you stay in that viewpoint from the beginning of the scene to the end. Occasionally an author mixes first person and third in a multiple viewpoint story, using the first person to signal the protagonist's scenes.

- **Omniscient point of view.** Here the author is not only the narrator but becomes, in a sense, the viewpoint character as well. The author does not actually appear in the story, of course, but describes the events based on his knowledge of the characters, events, and issues with which the story deals. Because the author knows everything (that's what omniscient means), there are no restrictions. You can describe what's going on at every place and at every moment. You can be inside every character's head, showing each individual's observations, thoughts, feelings, and actions.

  The omniscient viewpoint may appear to be the easiest to handle, but it has its own pitfalls. It can sometimes degenerate into an attempt to give everyone's point of view at once. Jump around too much from one character's head to another, and your readers are likely to become distracted or befuddled rather than enlightened. *The Life of the Party* on page 53 is deliberately presented this way to provide a basis for writing exercises. Read it as an example of the omniscient viewpoint misused.

This approach can also be more distancing. Readers may have difficulty figuring out which character to identify with. The author's commentary, coming from beyond the story, can seem intrusive, pulling readers out of the moment and destroying the immediacy of the story. The omniscient viewpoint requires skill and care equal to the others.

■ **Limited omniscient viewpoint.** This sounds like a contradiction in terms. How can you be limited if you know everything? I tend to think of it as the ten-degrees-over viewpoint: While we as readers are inside the character's head, we are also outside of it, standing about ten degrees away. With this approach the writer allows us to discern subtleties about the character that would not come through in a strictly limited first person narrative:

> The first call came on Wednesday evening as Dorothy Ann washed up the plate and pot she'd used for her supper. Through the small, square window over the sink she was watching the last streak of orange fade from the sooty sky.
> At the the third ring she sighed, dropped the sudsy rag into the water and shuffled over to the phone on the far kitchen wall. "Hello," she said into the black receiver.
> "I love you," said the voice at the other end.
> "Hello?" she repeated. "Who is this?" But the only response was a click and the dial tone's buzz.

Dorothy Ann is the sole viewpoint character in this story. The reader sees the events only from her perspective; we never hear another character's thoughts except as they are expressed out loud to Dorothy Ann herself. Yet at the same time that readers are in her head, listening to her thoughts, we are seeing her from a slight remove. Take the shuffle in her gait, for instance;

we notice it, but it is unlikely that she herself thinks of her walk in quite that way.

THREE TIPS FOR HANDLING OF POINT OF VIEW

Whether you choose first person or one of the variants of third person, keeping the following points in mind will help you handle point of view effectively:

- **Be consistent.** Once you choose a viewpoint character for a scene, stick with that person. An inadvertent shift in the point of view can weaken the impact.

  When you place your readers inside a character's head, be sure that what we see, hear, feel, and think is what the character can see, hear, feel, and think. The viewpoint character generally can't see the expression on her own face, or read another person's mind, so readers can't either.

- **Keep the character in character.** A character's inner monologue—his expression of his thoughts—should echo the tone, attitude, and vocabulary that he uses when speaking out loud. When he draws the readers' attention to something, it should be the kind of detail that he would be expected to notice, given the person he is. Walking into a restaurant, an artist's eye might be drawn first to the color scheme or the paintings on the walls; his companion, the society queen, focuses on spotting the important people present. Mary is impressed with the lobster *aux épinards*, but Albert wishes he could trade in all this frou-frou food for a decent plate of fried clams. Gloria, on the other hand, hardly notices the food, the decor, or the other diners; she's too busy fretting about whether she has enough cash in her wallet to pay for her dinner.

- **When in doubt, try a different point of view.** Just as your choice of protagonist isn't always obvious, neither is your choice of point of view. If you are having trouble writing a story, experiment with the point of view. Shifting from third person to first can give you deeper insight into your protagonist or narrator, while switching from first to third can open up a story and provide greater opportunities to bring various characters into play.

Bringing Your Characters to Life

Meeting new and interesting people is one of the great pleasures of reading—and writing—fiction. Our favorite characters take on lives of their own. In a novel, when we have more time to spend with them, they come to seem like friends. One mark of a successful book is the reluctance of readers to part company with characters we've grown fond of.

In a short story, you don't have sufficient space to let your readers establish long-term relationships with your characters. Yet the sense that the characters are real people, that they are truly alive if only in some alternate universe, adds immeasurably to our willingness to become involved in the story and to let it affect us in the way you intended. If we believe in your characters, we will believe in the rest of the story. If the characters strike us as wooden figures, or wind-up toys, or chess pieces you're pushing around on a board, we will resist getting involved; we may even quit reading.

Some characters are so vividly drawn that they walk out of their stories and into the popular imagination, becoming cultural archetypes. Sherlock Holmes, Charles Dickens' miserly Ebenezer Scrooge, and James Thurber's daydreaming Walter Mitty are well known to people who have never read the stories in which they appeared.

To create characters who become real, you must know them intimately. The better you know them, the easier it will be for you to bring them to life for the reader. You won't put everything you know on the page; there's not room for that, nor is there any need. But when you know exactly who they are, what they think, how they feel, how they act and react, you can be confident that what does appear on the page is right. Your characters will help you tell the story in the strongest, most effective way.

Getting to know them isn't an instantaneous process. Achieving intimate knowledge of any new acquaintance takes time, effort, and a willingness on your part to be open.

Some writers write biographical sketches of their characters before they begin a story. Others make charts to keep track of pertinent details. A sample of such a chart appears on page 41.

If you'd like to try this system, you can use it as is or let it inspire a more helpful one of your own.

Some writers, though, find it hard to get to know a character in advance in this way. We need to see them walking around in the story, flexing their muscles. We need to hear them speak and watch them respond to what other characters say and do. For me, going through this get-acquainted process is one of the main purposes of a first draft.

When my novel *A Relative Stranger* was in the planning stage, I wrote extensive biographical notes for only one character, a private investigator named O'Meara whom I expected to play a key role in the book. I could see the man clearly—tall, lanky, with shaggy brown hair that glinted reddish in the sun. He was a law school dropout who lived in San Francisco, and both of these facts dismayed his family, ambitious Texas politicians who had had far different plans for him. When I began writing, I knew O'Meara much better than any other character in the book.

There was only one problem: When I placed him in the story, he folded his arms and refused to perform. By the time I finished the first draft, he appeared in only a single scene. The most obvious alternatives were to shoehorn him into scenes he didn't belong in or to get rid of him.

My solution? I turned O'Meara into an Irish setter. He was clearly happier to be a dog. Once I made the switch, the second draft proceeded much more smoothly. O'Meara came to life at last, wagging his tail, and settled comfortably into the story. Perhaps the other O'Meara, the man I thought I knew so well, will find a place in another story.

You'll need to experiment to discover how and when your characters come alive for you. You may find that it changes from story to story, and from character to character.

Whether your characters have become old friends by the time you launch into your first draft or still are strangers, here are five techniques that will help you achieve an intimate acquaintance with them and bring them to life for your readers.

I. MAKE THEM THREE-DIMENSIONAL.

For a solid object, the three dimensions are length, width, and depth. These define the way the object occupies space. But the only space a fictional character occupies is a corner of the author's mind. A character is a fantasy, a mere wisp of thought.

Lajos Egri, author of the classic work, *The Art of Dramatic Writing*, defined the three dimensions of fictional characters as physical, sociological, and psychological. This concept can help you create imaginary people who seem as solid as they would if they were real:

- **Physical.** When we meet someone new, the details of his appearance are the source of our first impressions. But the physical dimension goes beyond the basics of size, shape, and coloring to include the state of his health, his body language and style of movement, and his mode of dress.

- **Sociological.** The sociological dimension encompasses the character's connections to the world—his family, his social status, his educational attainments, his profession, his regional, ethnic, cultural, and socioeconomic background, and his relationships with other people.

- **Psychological.** The character's basic personality fits into the psychological dimension—his temperament and outlook on life, his passions and talents, his sense of humor, and his emotions, including his hopes and fears.

Just as people who live in the real world have multifaceted lives, so do people who populate the realms of fiction. The Tip Sheet: Three-Dimensional Characters on page 39 delves deeper into these three dimensions, giving you some questions to ask your characters as you get acquainted with them and come to understand their complexities.

2. GIVE THEM A PAST AND A FUTURE.

A character does not begin to exist at the opening moment of the story. She has had a life, perhaps many years long. How has she come to be in this particular place at this instant in time?

The answer to this question is sometimes called the back story—in other words, the story that lies behind the one you are telling and provides a context for it. The back story is constructed out of the circumstances of the characters' three-dimensional lives. It includes their key relationships, their formative experiences and memory-making moments. Obviously you won't include all these details in your story; you may not even be aware of some of the back story except subconsciously. The points from the back story that come forward into your current narrative should be those that have a bearing on the present events. But knowing the back story will help you understand your characters and their current behavior and give them extra depth.

Just as you want to give readers the sense that your characters have their own rich history, you want us to feel that they will continue to live once the story is over. For your central character especially, the story provides a stepping stone from the past into the future. The events that transpire should have an effect on her, changing her in some way, causing her to learn or grow. Depending on the story, the change could be small, almost unnoticeable, or it could be huge—anything from a brief flicker of insight to a shift in a relationship to a major alteration of lifestyle. At the end of the story the protagonist is not quite the same person she was when it began.

For every character, even minor ones, try to create the impression that he or she has an existence beyond the confines of the page. Readers should believe in the possibility that an interesting story could be built around any one of them; this just happens to be the story you're choosing to tell for now.

3. GIVE THEM EMOTIONS AND CONTRADICTIONS.

What is most telling about characters is not the details about their lives and personalities; it's how they feel about those details. Their thoughts and emotions are what truly define them. For example:

Susan is 45 years old. Is there another age she'd rather be? Does she regret no longer being young, or does she feel she is blossoming now that her children are grown?

Michael stands almost six and a half feet tall. Does he enjoy being that height? Does he take advantage of his power to intimidate shorter people? Does he resent being asked yet again, "How's the weather up there?" or being told that he must be great at basketball?

Victor lives in a large colonial house in a posh suburb. What would he change about the place if he had a choice? Is this home the fulfillment of a long-held dream, or does he miss his small, easy-care apartment and the excitement of his old neighborhood in the city?

Anna is a plumber. Does she enjoy her job? Does she feel successful at it? What made her choose this line of work? Would she choose it again if she had to start over?

Some authors try to rely on character tags, hoping these will substitute for the serious work of really getting to know the person in question: *Hey, I've got a great idea. I'll write about a one-legged accountant from Arizona who raises parrots.* This is fine as a starting point, but it's not enough to carry the story. What counts is *why* the person is the way he is, and how he is affected by it. Unless such identification tags are developed, the character becomes a mere stage prop.

Nor can you simply assign characters roles as good guys or bad. None of us is all vice or all virtue. Often our motives and actions seem ambiguous and contradictory, even to ourselves. We act in ways that undermine our own stated intentions (*...really, I meant to stick to my diet, but there was this cherry-cheese danish, just calling to me...*). Our hearts convince us of one thing even as our heads tell us the opposite. Sometimes we must choose one course or the other, even though we are uncertain which way would be best.

Our emotions—love, loyalty, greed, jealousy, hate, fear—are the source of our strongest and most revealing motivations and actions. Feelings have no logic attached to them. This is what gives us our color, our edge, our quirkiness.

All of this applies to fictional characters too. To ring true to readers, characters need to have some complexities and contradictions in their makeup. It is as difficult for us to relate to a flawless hero as to a villain with no redeeming qualities. We all have dark sides and light sides to our natures, and the stories that speak to both are the ones we find most rewarding.

4. MAKE THEM ACT BELIEVABLY.

Characters who act out of character undermine a story's hard-won credibility. They make it hard for readers to maintain their willing suspension of disbelief. The behavior of your characters will be believable if it meets these five tests:

■ **It is consistent.** Despite all the ambiguities and contradictions in their nature, people tend to behave in consistent ways, based on who they are physically, psychologically, and sociologically. They operate on the basis of habit and take comfort from routines. This is true even of those who pride themselves on being nonconformist; their patterns of behavior may be unconventional but they are patterns nonetheless. If a character in your story does behave strangely or inconsistently, he should have a strong reason for doing so, and someone inside the story (not just your readers) should notice.

■ **It fits the character's motivation.** Each character in your story has some sort of personal agenda—a goal to achieve or a desire to attain. This is what motivates her actions. As we will see in the next chapter, these varying agendas are the source of the conflict that drives the events of the story. Characters act to further their own self-interest, whatever they perceive that to be.

■ **It arises from his emotions as well as his intellect.** As noted earlier, people's most powerful actions arise out of their emotions.

■ **It balances the risk and the payoff.** Believability problems often arise because what the character will gain from a course of action is not worth the risk it entails. Most people would not rush into a burning house in order to retrieve a favorite sweater, but they would to rescue a child. Now suppose what's inside the house is the only existing copy of a manuscript that represents five years of intense work? The character will have to decide whether the payoff merits the risk—and then convince us he's right.

■ **It doesn't require your character to be a fool.** Sometimes, in order to move the story in a certain direction, you may be tempted to have a usually sensible character act like an idiot. Think of the B movies in which the heroine, instead of going for help, tiptoes down the stairs all alone into the cellar where the lights have been mysteriously extinguished so she can investigate those disturbing screams. The risk is that you will lose your readers' sympathy, and there is little payoff in that.

This is the time to put your imagination into high gear, play plenty of "what if...," and come up with a better solution.

5. SHOW THEM IN ACTION.

When we're getting acquainted with friends, neighbors, classmates, or coworkers, we don't do so by reading their bios. We come to know them through what they tell us about themselves, what other people say about them, and what we observe about their behavior. With characters in a story, the readers' strongest relationships are formed in these same ways, with an added bonus: In the case of viewpoint characters, we can listen to their thoughts.

Providing a background summary is the easiest but least effective way to give readers information about a character. What we can see and hear for ourselves is much more powerful than anything the author explains to us. It's like the difference between having a friend describe the blind date she's arranged for us and actually arriving at the restaurant and meeting the touted stranger.

Because you have the limited space in a short story, you may need to give us a few details in summary. But as much as you can, reveal the character through:

What she does: How she acts and reacts.

What he thinks: How he talks to himself in his own inner monologue.

What she says: How she expresses herself in dialogue with other characters.

What others think and say: What they say to him directly, and how they discuss him in his absence.

Here's an example, in which we meet a young woman named Christine. The segments are in the reverse of the order above:

What others say about her: "I don't see how Christine can turn down a nice young man like Jack," her mother said.

"I guess she just doesn't want to marry him," said her father.

"Well, she did before. I mean, they've been engaged for six months."

"She changed her mind. Woman's prerogative."

"It's not like she'll have many more chances. She's twenty-six. And men as nice as Jack don't come along every day. Soon they'll all be snapped up by the sensible girls and who'll be left for Christine? Just the misfits and the failures and the woman-haters."

"Now, Fran, she's an attractive, sensitive young woman," her father said. "She'll have no problem finding as many young men as she wants when she decides she wants them."

"This is serious, George," insisted her mother "What can we do to make her change her mind?"

"Nothing. We haven't been able to make her change her mind since the time she decided to be born three weeks early and ruined our plans for a last quiet weekend at the beach."

"Well, I'd like to see her settled down. And I wouldn't even mind seeing a grandchild or two come along one of these days."

"I don't know, Fran. I'm too young to be a grandfather just yet. Besides, I suspect Wendy and Richard will decide to tie the knot before long."

"That's just what I mean. Here's her baby sister ready to get married when we haven't got Christine to the altar yet. And think about poor Jack. You know how much in love with her he is. And he's such a fine young man."

"Then it won't be long until some fine young woman snaps him up. Christine will settle down when she's good and ready, just like she does everything else. If she marries Jack to please you or me, or Jack himself for that matter, she'll be miserable. It's something she has to decide for herself."

What she says: "It's got nothing to with Jack," Christine told Wendy. "I really do love him. But he's ready to settle down and buy a house and have a baby, and I'm not. I want some travel and excitement first. It's as simple as that."

"Can't you travel and have excitement together?" Wendy asked. "That's what Richard and I plan to do."

"Jack got adventuring out of his system during those years when he dropped out of school. Now that he has his degree he's ready to conquer the corporate world. I don't care about the corporate world; I want to see the real one."

"You can't see much of the real one with only two weeks of vacation a year."

"I know. That's why I'm quitting my job."

"Quitting!"

"Yep. I'm giving notice on Friday. Don't tell Mom and Dad. I'd better spring it on them myself."

"Wow, what are you going to do?"

"I'm going to Hawaii for starters. Jennifer's in Honolulu now. She said I can stay with her while I look for a job and a place to live. Then when I get tired of that, I'll try someplace else. Maybe get a grant from the Australian government to go there for a couple of years."

"They only do that if you have some kind of skill they need."

"Well, who knows what they might need. It's worth checking into. Oh, Wendy, I can't wait!"

What she thinks: I'm so excited! Aloha, Hawaii! Aloha, Christine! If they hang a lei around my neck when I get off the plane, I hope it's a yellow one. Wonder what I should take. Just a suitcase—I can always send for stuff later. Or get new things. Wendy can use what's in my apartment.

What a relief to get that hunk of rock off my finger. The longer I wore it, the more it bothered me. I told Jack it was too big and fussy when he gave it to me. My hand's too small for a ring like that. But it had been his mother's, so that was that. If I do get married someday, I won't wear a wedding ring. Men don't a lot of the time and no one thinks a thing of it. Poor Jack. I know he's disappointed, but he'll get over it. Plenty of women will be champing at the bit to marry him. I bet Laurie Meissner's at his apartment right now putting in her application.

What she does: Christine lifted the red suitcase to the bed and opened it. What to put in it? The yellow daisy-print dress, of course; that would be neat and appropriate for job hunting. She took the dress from the closet and laid it out on the bed. She folded it neatly, twice lengthwise and once across its width, and placed it in the bottom of the suitcase.

She rolled up her old soft jeans and set them on the bed. From her third bureau drawer she took the yellow-and-blue bikini and the turquoise tank suit and stacked them on top of the jeans.

Back at the closet, reaching for the beige skirt and jacket, she spotted her wedding dress and pulled that out instead. She removed the dress from its protective plastic and held it up to her, kicking the closet door shut so she could admire herself in the full-length mirror that hung on it. Looking at herself she frowned, then draped the dress carefully over the bed. She swept her hairbrush through her long locks and dabbed on a bit of reddish lipstick. From the row of shoes at the bottom of the closet, she pulled the white sandals with heels and slipped them onto her bare feet. Then she held up the wedding dress in front of her again, smoothed its white skirt and twirled before the mirror.

"Christine? Can I help you, dear?" Her mother's voice from the hallway. Quickly, before Mom could come into the bedroom, Christine stuck the dress on its hanger and thrust it back into the closet. Spotting the plastic still lying on the bed, she balled it up and tossed it onto the closet floor.

Look how much we have learned about Christine simply from watching and listening, without needing any intervention from an outside narrator. We know that at age twenty-six she is breaking her engagement to a man named Jack; though fond of him, she's not yet ready to settle down. Even so, Christine is a sensible, steady young woman. She holds a job and has her own apartment. Her plans for the future include another job and apartment, albeit in a more exotic location. She is neat by nature (look at the carefully folded dress in the suitcase and the shoes lined up in a row on her closet floor). And despite what she's telling herself and others, her actions show that she is feeling a little bit ambivalent about her big decision.

We've learned about her family, too, which includes parents and a younger sister named Wendy who is also engaged. Her mother is dismayed by Christine's change of plans; her father is more supportive. We know that Jack dropped out of school for a long period but returned to earn a college degree; now he is launching a business career. An attractive man, he is what in Christine's mother's youth would have been known as a good catch.

That's just a sampling—there's more information to be gleaned from these paragraphs. What we don't know is whether in the end Christine leaves or stays.

Tip Sheet:
Three-Dimensional Characters

I. PHYSICAL CHARACTERISTICS

Body Type—Height, weight, build, coloring, features. How does the character feel about her physical self?

Health—What physical problems, if any, does the character experience? Does he consider them a major or a minor problem? How much do they interfere with his activities?

Clothing—What kinds of clothes and accessories does she typically wear? What does she feel most comfortable in? What is her personal style?

Movement—What is his style of movement? Is he graceful or awkward? An exercise nut or a couch potato?

2. SOCIOLOGICAL CHARACTERISTICS

Name—What name does she go by? Is it the name she was given at birth or one she chose for herself? Does she have a nickname? How are her age, her heritage, and her parents' expectations reflected in her name?

Basic Biographical Details—Age, when and where born, how he got from childhood to this point. What is his current attitude toward his earlier years?

Social Status, Cultural and Ethnic Background—How have these shaped her? Is she an insider or outsider in her current milieu?

Significant Relationships—Parents, siblings, spouse, children, past and present lovers, friends. How have these people influenced or affected him? What is the state of their current relationships?

Residence—Town, neighborhood, type of abode. How does she feel about living there? What kind of environment has she created for herself in her personal spaces (home, office)?

Education—What type and how much? To what uses has his education been put? Was his education the kind he wanted or felt he deserved?

Occupation or Profession—What does she do for a living? Is she good at it? Does she find it enjoyable or rewarding? Is she happy with the status and remuneration it gives her? How is she thought of by her colleagues, superiors, and subordinates? Is she more comfortable in a secure job or is she an entrepreneurial type?

Religion, Superstitions, Social and Political Beliefs—What shapes his worldview? How serious a believer is he? How sincere? How tolerant or intolerant of others' views?

3. PSYCHOLOGICAL CHARACTERISTICS

Personality—What is his basic temperament and outlook on life? Is he an optimist or a pessimist? Outgoing or reclusive? Emotional or self-contained? Trusting or suspicious? Slow or quick to anger?

Speech Patterns—Is she articulate? Glib? Tongue-tied? What sort of jargon or slang does she use? Is there a regional flavor to her speech?

Attitude toward Self—What does he like and not like about himself? What does he count as his greatest successes and failures? How would he change himself? Does he see himself as others see him?

Talents, Interests, Passions—What is she especially good at? What does she love to do, or to have? What would be her perfect day?

Habits and Routines—How does he get through a typical day? How does he respond if his regular routines are interrupted?

Response to Stress—Does she fall apart in a crisis? Come through it fine and then fall apart? Not notice the crisis? Create the crisis in the first place?

Humor—What makes him laugh? What kind of jokes does he tell?

Hot Buttons—What drives her crazy? What are her pet peeves?

Attitude toward the Opposite Sex—And attitude toward sex in general. How did these attitudes develop?

Attitude toward Authority—Does he see the police, or his boss, or his parent, as friend or foe?

Fondest Dream and Darkest Fear—These can be strong motivating factors.

Character's Bio Chart

NAME:

Physical description:

Profession (what and where):

Description of residence:

Personality (attitudes, emotions, opinions, quirks, and habits):

Avocations and interests:

Background (parents, education, early life):

Current significant relationships:

Other important things to know about this person:

Giving Your Characters a Voice

Convincing, natural-sounding dialogue is one of the sharpest storytelling tools at your disposal. It can also be one of writing's toughest challenges, unless you happen to be blessed with an excellent ear for the nuances of how people speak. But your ear can be trained, and it's worth taking the time, effort, and care to learn to do dialogue well.

THE FUNCTIONS OF DIALOGUE

Dialogue is a form of action. It captures the attention of readers in the same way action does, and we take a certain pleasure in overhearing other people speak. Well-written dialogue serves three valuable functions in a story:

- **It reveals character.** Of the four ways to present a character to your readers, two of them involve dialogue and a third, inner monologue, also requires giving your character his own particular voice.

- **It provides information.** It's fine for the writer to tell readers what's going on, but it can be even more effective and engaging to have the characters do it. When the characters speak, we remain firmly in the time and place of the story, without being pulled away for an authorial explanation. One caution: The conversation will sound stilted if you have your characters tell each other details they already know just for your readers' benefit:

  "Your husband—you know, that guy Robert Brown who works in the shipping department?—he tried to pick a fight with me today."

  "Mrs. Snyder, your sixth grade teacher, said to tell you the homework is due on Friday, the last day of the school week."

- **It moves the story forward.** Dialogue is more than gossip or idle chitchat. What the characters tell each other, and the readers, should be pertinent to the story and help to keep its momentum rolling.

When a friend phones you, you recognize without being told that it's Jim on the line and not Harry. Even before you peek at the signature on a letter, you can tell from the way she describes events that it came from Karen and not Melissa.

Everyone sounds different. Not only does the sound of the voice have unique qualities—high-pitched or low, breathy, raspy, musical—but the words we choose and the way we string them together are individual as well.

Listen to the three characters below. Each one is conveying the same information to the same man but doing so in his or her own personal style:

Paul: "Excuse me, Mr. Honeycut, sir, but please do partake of some of this lovely chocolate mousse. I think you will find it suitably delicious. And Pierre assures me that it is not fattening."

Anthony: "Yo, Honeycut! Hey man, get yourself down with some of this chocolate mouse—I mean mousse. It's way cool—like ta-ays-tee! And guaranteed low-cal, too, man. You know that Pierre dude? He says so for sure."

Suzette: "Dessert time, Mr. Honeycut! And look what we've got for you! Chocolate mousse! Don't you just love chocolate? It's my very favorite food in the whole world. But here's the best part—Pierre says this is *skinny* chocolate mousse. So we can eat as much as we want and not feel one bit guilty. Isn't he just a dream of a cook?"

Without knowing any more about these people, their relationship to Mr. Honeycut, or the occasion at which the chocolate mousse is being served, you have probably already formed strong impressions of Paul, Anthony, and Suzette—their ages, their positions in life, their personalities, even what they look like.

Your job as the author of a story is to help each character find his or her own distinctive voice. Readers should be able to identify which character is speaking by his or her speech pattern. The more you can distinguish your characters by their manner of speaking, the more the reader will believe in them as real individuals.

This is trickier when your characters have a lot in common—when they come from the same region or socioeconomic background, have equivalent levels of education, or have similar hobbies or professions. But even people who are similar in most respects have their own habits and quirks when it comes to speaking.

Sometimes when you know your characters intimately, you come to hear their voices clearly in your head. Writing dialogue then becomes almost a matter of taking down their dictation. But writers are not always that lucky. Often we must work hard on a character's voice, first to hear it and then to reproduce it on the page.

One way to develop your ear is to engage in creative eavesdropping. When you are at work, at school, on a bus, in a cafe, listen closely to how the people you encounter express themselves. You're listening not for content but for the kinds of words and phrases they use and the rhythm and beat of their speech.

Use the Tip Sheet: Dialogue on page 49 to guide your listening and to give each character an individual voice.

BRINGING READERS INTO THE CONVERSATION

Though readers never get to put in our two cents' worth, you want us to participate in the scene, to be avidly watching and listening, when your characters speak to one another. As the conversational ball bounces back and forth, your first task is to lay out the spoken words on the page so it's clear who is speaking to whom, where they are, and what they're doing. Your second task is to step out of the way and let the characters speak for themselves. Let their words, not yours, convey what's going on. If you overexplain what's going on in the dialogue, your intrusion will be obvious and distracting.

The following techniques will help you accomplish both aims:

■ **Write "suggestive" dialogue.** This doesn't mean to include naughty jokes or double entendres. Rather, the idea is to create speech that sounds genuine but really isn't. If you've ever read a transcript of a tape-recorded conversation, you know that when it's set down on the page, real speech

44

becomes a confusing mishmash and a deadly bore. Real speech is useless as dialogue: It's too full of "uhs," repetitions, digressions, sentence fragments, and aimless prattle. Instead of replicating real speech, try to simulate it so it sounds convincing but is comprehensible and to the point. Remember, every line of dialogue should carry out one of the three functions described above.

■ **Keep your attributions clear and unobtrusive.** An attribution is a tag line that identifies the speaker. Here are some thoughts on handling them effectively:

Stick to the word "said." Most of the time you want to avoid using a word too frequently or at points too close together. *Said*, though, is an invisible word; the reader jumps over the verb to focus on the speaker's name. *Asked* works the same way for questions.

Sometimes it may be important to give the reader additional information about how the speaker says the words—*Joe called, whispered, muttered.* (Be careful, though, about *hissed.* Writers sometimes try to use it to suggest an angry whisper, but a hiss is in fact a prolonged *s* sound. You can't hiss words that don't contain an *s* or *z*.)

Said and *asked* have other tempting synonyms—*exclaimed, proclaimed, uttered, announced, expounded, expostulated*, and a host of others. Keep these to a minimum; they call attention to themselves, which distracts from the words the character is speaking.

Avoid adverbs and adjectives. For the same reason, you want to minimize the use of adjectives and adverbs—*angrily, sarcastically, softly, smirking, confused*—in your attributions. Let the character's own words convey the tone of voice so that readers can hear it correctly in their mental ears.

"You jerk! Get out of here!" Jane yelled angrily. "I never want to see you again."

Jane's wrath is obvious; adding the word *angrily* only hits us over the head with what we already know.

The exception—though it should occur rarely—is when the character's tone is contrary to what his words would lead you to expect:

"I'm going to break your neck," Miles said in his sweetest voice.

Skip the attribution altogether. Attributions serve two purposes—they pinpoint who the speaker is, and they provide information that is not contained in the character's own words. But they also slow the pace of the dialogue scene. Sometimes it's more effective to let the spoken words stand alone, using only occasional attributions to help readers keep track of who's speaking. For an example, look back at the dialogue sections of Christine's story.

Identify the speaker at the first opportunity. Unless the speech is very short, don't leave the attribution to the end. The most natural and easy-reading place to stick *he said* is at the first pause or breathing point in the speech. Usually this means after the first sentence or long phrase. That way the reader doesn't discover upon reaching the end of the paragraph that the person speaking is not who she thought it was.

Use only one attribution or tag per paragraph. Usually this is enough. If you've included *he said*, you don't need to add *he continued* later on. If the paragraph includes an action or gesture on the part of the speaker, that's a sufficient identifying tag, so you might not even need *he said*.

■ **Use stage business effectively.** The term *stage business*, borrowed from the theater, describes the actions a character makes while speaking—sipping coffee, twirling a wineglass by the stem, breaking a blossom off the bouquet and sniffing it, petting the dog, lighting a cigar, or whatever. Stage business has several functions in a dialogue scene. You can use stage business to:

Substitute for the attribution. You can signal who the speaker is without using *said* or one of its cousins.

Help set the scene. Stage business has the advantage of being more visual than a simple attribution. You can bring in sensory details to increase the you-are-there quality for the reader.

Break up long speeches or conversations. Yes, dialogue is action, but talking-head scenes—long stretches of dialogue during which nothing else happens—become static pretty quickly. Stage business makes such scenes livelier.

Signal a shift in the speaker's thought or tone. Placed in the middle of a speech, a line of stage business gives the speaker a graceful way to change the subject.

Characterize the speaker. When choosing stage business, think of activities that would be natural to the individual character, the time, and the place. Greg smokes too much; Lucy doodles dollar signs on a paper napkin.

Notice how stage business works in this exchange between a real estate agent and a couple who show up at a Sunday open house:

The woman meandered about the living room, running fingers over the furniture, picking up knickknacks, putting them down. Her doing that made me jittery; it wasn't the furniture that was for sale.

"Feel free to look around." I forced myself to sound cheerful. "It's a lovely house, very well priced for the neighborhood. Did you see our ad in the paper?"

"We saw the sign out front." The woman kept shifting from foot to foot in an awkward little jig, until I wanted to grab her and make her stand still. "We've kind of had our eyes on this house, haven't we, Hal?"

The man was still leaning against the archway in the foyer, hands hidden in the pocket of his wrinkled gray overcoat. "Furniture's all here," he said. His wife—or girlfriend?—had certainly established that.

"The van is coming this week for the Dunbars' things," I explained. "You could move in quite soon if you decide to buy."

"Buy what? Oh, you thought—"The woman picked up a silver candlestick from the mantel and rubbed a ragged fingernail along its rim. "See, we're old friends of Ray Dunbar's."

"Please put that down." I tried for tact. "This afternoon, the house is my responsibility. It's my fault if anything goes wrong."

"Huh? Oh, sure." She replaced the candlestick and began fiddling with a cigarette box. "It's strange, though—Ray never said anything about moving, did he, Hal?"

Hal hadn't budged from the archway. "C'mon. We better look around."

The woman bounced excitedly. "Yeah, let's go."

Body language—a person's gestures and movements—can be a useful part of stage business. But don't rely too much on having your characters lean forward, lean back, turn, shrug, smile, nod, or shake their heads. Too many motions like these can make the character come across as restless or jumpy. Moreover, they're hard to individualize: A shrug of the shoulders is a shrug whether Lucy's doing it or Greg. More purposeful actions add greater interest and vividness to dialogue scenes.

Use a period rather than a comma when you introduce a speech with an action. In other words: *Greg smiled. "Are you sure?"* rather than *Greg smiled, "Are you sure?"* It's possible to smile while you're speaking, but not to smile out loud.

■ **Give each person's speech its own paragraph.** In dialogue, readers expect a new paragraph to signal a change of speaker. You can avoid confusion by not putting lines from two people in the same paragraph. Similarly, hold your characters to one paragraph per speech and don't let them ramble on. If someone insists on being long-winded, you have three options:

Impose some discipline on him. In other words, shorten the speech.

Give him some stage business. Let him perform it at the start of the second paragraph, and include his name to clarify that he is still the one speaking.

Have the listener react at various points. She could ask a question, make a comment, prod for more information, express encouragement or skepticism, let out an expletive—whatever might lead the speaker to his next point. She need not respond out loud. An action, a gesture, or a silent thought might do as well, or even better if you want to keep the listener's reaction a secret from the speaker. Having the listener be responsive makes the exchange more of a dialogue and less of a monologue.

Tip Sheet: Dialogue

How to Give Your Characters Distinctive Voices

I. VARY THEIR DEGREE OF ARTICULATENESS.

Is this person:
- Glib? Tongue-tied?
- Verbose? Taciturn?
- Rambling? Direct and to the point?
- A user of filler words...*uh, ya know,* etc.?

2. VARY THE LENGTH AND STRUCTURE OF THEIR SENTENCES.

Does this person:
- Use short, clipped sentences? Run-on sentences?
- Drop words at the beginning of sentences?
- Use incomplete sentences—get halfway through and then switch gear into a new sentence?
- Fail to complete thoughts, but let them trail off?
- Interrupt a lot?

3. VARY THE LENGTH OF THEIR TYPICAL SPEECHES.

Does this person:
- Talk a lot or only a little bit?
- Like to volunteer lots of detail? Or require coaxing to speak at all?

4. VARY THEIR VOCABULARY.

Does this person:
- Sound educated or uneducated?
- Use long words or short words?
- Have an expansive vocabulary or a limited one?

5. GIVE CHARACTERS THEIR OWN EXCLAMATIONS, CURSE WORDS, AND PET EXPRESSIONS.

These tend to be very personal. We all have our favorites and they become ingrained, so we use them without thinking. Assign your characters their own, and let them be fairly consistent (though not boringly repetitive) in using these phrases.

Does this person:

- Take the Lord's name in vain? How? *"Oh God!" "My Lord!" "Jesus H. Christ!"*
- Curse vulgarly or mildly? How? *"Hell!" "Damn!" "Darn it!" "Phooey!!"*
- Use sensory tags? Which ones? *"You see..." "Listen up..." "I hear you..."*
- Have a habitual way to express agreement? *"Absolutely right." "Exactly." "No kidding." "You got that right."*
- Have other characteristic expressions that he or she uses routinely?

6. LET CHARACTERS USE SLANG, JARGON, AND REGIONAL OR ETHNIC EXPRESSIONS

Does this person:

- Use a little slang or a lot? What kind?
- Use professional jargon? (A doctor uses different words than a computer hacker or a cop.)
- Use expressions common to the region where he or she lives or grew up?
- Speak with a dialect and accent? (These can be tricky to get right. It's better to hint at it rather than try to replicate it with unconventional spellings and usages that can make dialogue hard to read.)

7. VARY THEIR APPROACH TO GRAMMAR AND THEIR LEVEL OF FORMALITY

Does this person:

- Speak ungrammatically? Speak with very proper grammar? (Most people fall in between.)
- Use contractions? (Not using contractions sounds stiff. It can suggest a non-native speaker.)

8. VARY THE KINDS OF INFORMATION THEY IMPART

Does this person:

- Speak openly about his or her emotions and personal life?
- Deflect personal talk and stick to impersonal matters?
- Love to gossip? Hate to gossip?
- Speak in "footnotes," providing lots of extraneous facts and figures?

Exercises: Creating Characters

1. Choose three short stories to read and think about. For each story, write brief answers to the following questions:

   a. Who is the protagonist? Why do you think the author chose to make this person the central character?

   b. How does the author handle the point of the view?

   c. Which characters in these stories seem to be the most three-dimensional, and why?

   d. How does the author work in the back story?

   e. What techniques does the author use to convey the characters to the reader?

2. Create a character and introduce him or her through four brief scenes, each using one of the following methods. Try to keep the author's voice out of the narrative. Let the readers see and hear the character directly:

   Scene 1: Through his or her own inner monologue.

   Scene 2: Through two people discussing the character in his or her absence.

   Scene 3: Through a dialogue between the character and another person.

   Scene 4: Through action, showing the character in a typical situation such as driving a car, getting dressed, or preparing a meal.

3. Read *The Life of the Party* on page 53 and then:

   a. *Character development:* Write a brief sketch describing one of the five people mentioned—Spanner, Maria, James, Alison, or Gary. Bring in his or her physical, sociological, and psychological characteristics.

   b. *Point of view:* Rewrite the scene above from the point of view of one of the five characters. Use first or third person, but remember that we are looking at what's happening strictly through this person's eyes. Feel free to add details; you don't need to stick to the events described.

Then choose a second character and rewrite the scene from this new person's point of view.

c. *Dialogue:* Write two separate dialogues in which one of the characters discusses the incident at the party with someone who was not there. For example:

- Maria talking to her mother.
- James talking to his therapist.

4. Write three brief scenes, each depicting one of the following situations entirely in dialogue. Characterize the speakers only through their words and their individual modes of expression, without any details of setting, action, or other background:

Scene 1: One person is trying to hide an opinion or feeling from the other. First, have the person succeed. Then rewrite the scene so that he or she fails.

Scene 2: Someone is telling two friends about finding a knapsack filled with cash in the woods. One friend wants to convince the first person to take the money to the police. The other friend tries to persuade the finder to keep it.

Scene 3: Three relatives are congratulating a bride at her wedding reception. One of them is in love with the groom and bitter that he's married someone else. Another dislikes the groom intensely and doesn't expect the marriage to last a year. The third genuinely wishes the young couple happiness.

5. Someone is telling a friend about attending a lavish dinner last Saturday night at the exclusive Greenwood Heights Country Club. The event was a fund-raiser for the governor's reelection campaign, and the narrator had the privilege of shaking the governor's hand. Write three scenes depicting this situation, changing the speaker each time:

Scene 1: A social climber who loves to go to parties, the fancier the better, and who becomes ga-ga over anybody famous.

Scene 2: A newspaper reporter who has to attend events like this all the time and finds them dull and boring.

Scene 3: An ambitious local politician who is maneuvering into position for a run at a higher office.

The Life of the Party

The party was full of noisy, unpleasant people, and Spanner was eager to get out of there until he saw Maria come in with James. Very nice, he thought as he watched her stroll across the room.

Maria noticed him staring at her and immediately was attracted to him. She abandoned James at the bar, leaving him feeling sullen and resentful as he ordered his first gin and tonic of the evening. She walked up to Spanner and smiled, trying hard to charm him.

Alison watched them with dismay. She'd been optimistic at the start of the evening, but now, seeing the sparks fly between Spanner and Maria, her hopes were dashed.

Gary was alarmed by the encounter too. "Uh-oh, there's going to be trouble," he muttered as he dug his pen and his palm-sized notebook out of his pocket.

Spanner and Maria, enjoying each other's company, were oblivious to the hateful looks Alison was giving them.

James noticed, though. He sidled over to Gary. "Wanna make a deal?" he asked.

Chapter 3

Conflict

How to Devise a Story
That Readers Won't Want to Put Down

To create a story, pick up your protagonist by the scruff of the neck and drop her headlong into a conflict.

Most of us try to avoid conflict in our lives, or so we contend. Yet without conflict we would have no challenges to meet, no obstacles to overcome, no victories to declare. Life would be easy, with happy outcomes assured. But it would also be flat, dull, and boring.

So it is with a story. Without conflict a story has no fuel, nothing to propel it forward, and no reason for readers to keep turning the pages. Throw in a bit of a struggle, and your narrative gains purpose and direction. You set up questions and issues that must be resolved. Now you have the energy, tension, and suspense to catch and keep our interest.

Conflict involves any two forces that are working in opposition. You're not required to fill your story with bloody battlefields or screaming matches or duels to the death. When the playground clique shuts a child out of a game, or two officemates are contending for promotion to the same higher position, conflict is brewing.

You don't even need to treat the conflict seriously. Look at P.G. Wodehouse's very funny tales, wherein the hapless English aristocrat Bernie Wooster constantly gets into scrapes, obliging his sensible valet Jeeves to bail him out. Remember, though, that in comedy it's the author and the readers who find the situation humorous. For the characters, there are critical issues at stake.

One way to test the viability of a story idea is to examine it for its potential for conflict. As you play the "what if..." game, look for three ways the situation could create a problem for a character or lead to a contest, a quarrel, or a misunderstanding. Identifying one possible conflict is sufficient, of course, but striving for three stretches your imagination farther. Often your second or third idea turns out to be the one that ignites your passion for the story.

How Conflict Works in a Short Story

Here's another definition: A story is "a description of what happens when a character attempts to overcome a conflict in order to achieve a goal or solve a problem." Character and conflict are the essence of what a story is about. One way to present it graphically is this:

```
                         C
                         O
                         N
                         F
CHARACTER  →  →  →  →  L  →  →  →  GOAL
                         I
                         C
                         T
```

Conflict is simply whatever is keeping your protagonist from getting what she wants in this situation. If your lead character has an ideal situation at the outset, or makes smooth, uninterrupted progress toward attaining it, that's wonderful, but it's not a story. The story occurs when the rocks appear in the road.

THREE KEY QUESTIONS

To figure out what kind of conflict your protagonist is facing, ask her these three questions. The answers are the keys to her motivation and will drive her actions throughout the story:

■ **What does she want to accomplish in the course of this story?** Just like any real person, a story character has desires and goals, things she yearns to obtain or achieve—love, money, justice, recognition, to hide a secret, to be popular, to conquer the mountain, to win the game, to land a better job, to escape the ghetto, to get out of a jam, to right a wrong, to protect herself or a loved one from danger. She has needs she must fill and dreams she hopes will come true. The protagonist becomes involved in the story for one reason: She perceives that the situation at hand will help her or hinder her in reaching an important goal.

■ **What is at stake?** If the protagonist reaches her goal, her success will have consequences. So will her failure if she falls short. In either case, other people in her life will also be affected, whether for good or ill. What does the protagonist expect these results to be, and how much do they matter to her? How far is she willing to go to ensure the outcome she hopes for or to avoid an unfavorable one?

■ **Who or what gets in her way?** This is where the conflict comes in. The protagonist encounters challenges and difficulties as she struggles to achieve her goal. Some may be imposed on her by outside forces she can't control; others may derive from her own desires and shortcomings.

Ask your other characters these questions too. Conflict arises when the goals of two characters are at cross-purposes. Every character has, to a greater or lesser degree, a vested interest in the situation depicted in the story. Each of them will try to turn the situation to his own best advantage, just as people do in real life. The only exceptions might be those who have the most minor of walk-on parts, who function like props in a scene—for example, the waitress who pours the coffee at the restaurant, or the bystanders gathered around watching the fistfight.

As the characters interact, their separate goals will either mesh or clash. How they respond when this happens becomes the basis of your plot.

The Protagonist's Predicament

Let's look more closely at the protagonist and her goal, because your story rides on her shoulders. She has the primary responsibility for drawing us into the story and keeping us there. To merit our time and attention, she must be someone we identify with and care about, and her predicament must move us to some level of concern.

Here are three ways to help her fulfill her obligation to the story.

1. MAKE THE GOAL A COMPELLING ONE.

A capricious whim won't do as a goal. Give your main character a mission that is meaningful, even life-changing, with significant consequences if she succeeds or fails. After all, you're about to put her through a certain amount of grief. She must have a strong reason to put up with it.

Readers should have a clear sense of the protagonist's goal at the beginning and throughout the narrative. She needn't announce it loudly. She may not even have great insight about it; she could be muddled or confused or self-deluded, as we all are at times. Her purpose might change in response to events that occur. But through her actions and reactions, her words and her thoughts, her goal should become apparent to us.

Don't forget to look at the goal behind the goal. What people say—or think—they want often is not the real issue. The underlying *why* can be even more important. Thomas's ambition to become a doctor may hide his true desire, which is to prove to his father that he is not a bumbling fool after all. Andrea may be desperate to marry Jeff because she loves him, as she proclaims, but perhaps what she really wants is to escape the violence or poverty or emotional coldness of her parents' home. The goal may appear to be a rational decision, and it may indeed make sense for purely logical reasons. But when it stems from a deep-seated emotional need or an unhealed wound, it can add a richer dimension to the character and to the story.

Note that the character's goal is not the same as the story goal that we discussed in Chapter One. The story goal is what is motivating you, the author. The character's goal is hers alone.

2. SET UP CHALLENGING ROADBLOCKS AND OBSTACLES.

When the protagonist encounters barricades in her path, our interest quickens. What will she do—climb over them or trip

58

over them? Suddenly the outcome is in doubt, the tension is heightened, and we become eager to find out what happens next.

In my short story, *The Hitchhiker*, a middle-aged woman named Carol, unaccustomed to traveling by herself, is driving to a distant city. Having just ended her marriage, her goal is a safe, uneventful journey to the place where she will begin her new life. But she complicates things for herself when, lonely and restless, she impulsively picks up a shaggy young man with his thumb out. Her imagination starts clicking and her quiet ride is over:

> One heard such awful stories about hitchhikers... Carol noticed her knuckles were white, she was gripping the wheel so tightly. She took ten deep breaths; usually that helped her relax. He'd been in the car for ten whole minutes and nothing had happened. Her handbag was safe beneath her seat...
>
> "Are you a student?" Carol asked. There were a lot of colleges scattered through this part of the state.
>
> "Nope, a working man."
>
> "Oh? What do you do?"
>
> He drummed his fingers on the armrest. "Odd jobs. Nothing interesting."
>
> I might find it very interesting, thought Carol, but she didn't press. Perhaps she was better off not knowing. He could be a house painter, an auto mechanic, something like that. Or a cocaine dealer, snickered a little voice inside her head. A hired killer.

It's been said that the author's job is to get the main character in trouble and then get her in worse trouble. In fact, this is the protagonist's whole reason for being. The word comes from the Greek: *proto* means "first, or chief"; *agonistes* means "to engage in combat"; thus, the protagonist is the story's number one combatant. The word *agony* derives from a related root, and conflict is what puts *agony* into *protagonist*.

It can be hard to make life for your main character as difficult as it needs to be. Chances are, you're fond of this person. She's someone you'd enjoy having as a friend. Perhaps she is you in disguise, her mask only the thinnest of veils. You don't want to be a bully or torturer, inflicting deliberate pain on either your friend or yourself. No doubt you're a nice person— gentle, polite, and kind. It goes against your nature to be mean.

Do it anyway. A common reason why short stories don't work is that the author pulls his punches. He refuses to let the protagonist confront and deal with the challenges that face her. In trying to soften the blows, the author diminishes the conflict and unintentionally robs the story of its tension and energy. The issues of the story go unresolved, and readers are left feeling unsatisfied.

3. PROVIDE A WORTHY OPPONENT.

You don't have a conflict if it's a foregone conclusion that the good guy's gonna win. The problems your main character confronts should be a true test of her mettle, exposing her shortcomings and calling forth her strengths.

Just as readers need someone to cheer for, we need someone or something to root against. The opponent should be as clever as the protagonist and have as much at stake. The more advantages an adversary enjoys over her—more power, more allies, more knowledge of what's going on—the greater are the tension and suspense.

Bad Guys, Hurricanes, and Fatal Flaws

This brings us to a consideration of the kinds of conflicts and opposing forces your characters might face. What could get in the way of the protagonist's reaching her goal? The possibilities are as limitless as your imagination. Frequently the opponent is another character, but not always. Your main character may face impersonal adversaries—events and circumstances that threaten to thwart her efforts to achieve her goal. She could even prove to be her own worst enemy.

For example, in Bharati Mukherjee's story, *The Management of Grief*, the world of the main character, Shaila, is thrown into upheaval when a plane crash claims the lives of her husband and sons. Shaila's goal is to find some way to come to terms with such an overpowering loss and to move, step by step, into what will become her new life. Her opponents are her own grief and the expectations that others hold about how she should feel and express it.

There are four principal types of conflict you can draw upon to set up your story's central struggle and provide the snags and impediments the protagonist must encounter as she tries to resolve it. Three are external, inflicted on her from outside sources. The fourth kind emanates from within. The richest stories develop when internal and external conflicts play against each other. An external conflict sets up a challenge. Does the character meet it with her strengths or her weaknesses? Either way, but particularly in the latter case, she could be setting the stage for a new problem to appear.

1. CONFLICT WITH ANOTHER PERSON

The protagonist may be opposed directly by another individual or a group of persons. In life we may think of such a person as an enemy, a rival, or simply a pain in the neck. In fiction he is the antagonist (from the Greek *anti,* meaning "against").

The protagonist and antagonist may at some level represent good versus evil. In a classic mystery story, for instance, the detective, on the side of law and justice, may match wits with a diabolic criminal. In Stephen Vincent Benét's *The Devil and Daniel Webster*, a New Hampshire farmer who has made a bad bargain enlists the celebrated nineteenth-century orator and statesman to take on the Devil himself.

More often, though, the antagonist is not someone we would normally think of as a villain. Often he is a friend, a colleague, a family member—someone who does not really intend to do the protagonist harm, or at least no more than is necessary to achieve his own goal. *Two Kinds*, a story from Amy Tan's *The Joy Luck Club*, portrays a daughter's battle with her mother, at first over piano lessons and ultimately over what a mother-daughter relationship should be. Although the girl certainly views her mother as an opposing force, there is love between them, and the woman is convinced that she is acting in her child's best interest.

2. CONFLICT WITH A FORCE OF SOCIETY

Your protagonist's fiercest battles may be those she wages against some condition of the society in which she lives: a war, a blighted neighborhood, prejudice, or social or cultural expectations that run counter to her goal.

The barriers that such conditions erect can be powerful and intimidating, and the consequences of trying to break through them can be profound. Societal forces could inspire you to satire and comedy or to drama and tragedy, depending on your personal attitudes, experiences, and perceptions.

Cynthia Ozick's chilling yet poetic story, *The Shawl*, brings home the horror of a Nazi death camp by showing a mother struggling to protect and nurture her children. The horror is pervasive yet impersonal; Ozick never dignifies it by giving it a human face. Sometimes, though, an author chooses to personify the social force, assigning a particular character or set of characters to represent the abstraction. When you do this, remember that to be convincing, these people still must be fully realized individuals—three-dimensional people with histories, emotions, contradictions, agendas, and goals. The concept they embody is only one part of their complex natures.

3. CONFLICT WITH A FORCE OF NATURE

Nature offers a convenient boon to writers—a wealth of dramatic possibilities in the form of mountains, deserts, jungles, oceans, drought, heat, ice, and storms. To make life rougher for a character, pour rain on her parade.

When the story's central conflict sets the protagonist against a force of nature, that force becomes the antagonist. The cliff she must climb or the blizzard she must survive functions as a character in the story. However, this doesn't mean you should anthropomorphize it; in other words, don't give it human characteristics, such as motives or emotions or personality. The power that forces of nature exert, and the fascination and terror they often hold for us, comes in part from the fact that they are emotionless. They have no will that we can, through art or cunning, bend to our own.

To Build a Fire by Jack London recounts a man's winter journey by foot through the Yukon wilderness from one remote camp to another. Although he thinks from time to time about people he knows, there is no other character in the story but a half-wild dog. Yet the man must pit his wits against a potent adversary—the extraordinary and relentless arctic cold.

4. CONFLICTS WITHIN ONESELF

We are our own worst enemies. No one can stymie our efforts to achieve a goal as effectively as we can ourselves.

Internal conflicts derive from factors inside us, from our own personality and emotions, particularly our faults and fears. They occur when two aspects of ourselves pitch a battle to control our actions. Our fears are especially skilled and sneaky fighters; they often foil our best-laid plans and strongest intentions. One example of an internal conflict is a writer's fight with the infernal internal editor when she sits down to start writing a story.

In classical tragedy the agent that caused the downfall of the protagonist was his own *hamartia*, his fatal flaw. This weakness or frailty of the personality—whether arrogance, pride, ambition, ambivalence, or bad judgment—would lead him to take an action or not take one, with disastrous consequences. It works much the same way in comedy, which is tragedy that has been stood on its head and given a happier ending.

A protagonist's struggle should involve both her good points and bad. At the same time she is using her skills, wits, and fortitude to overcome certain problems, her own failings are creating or compounding others. Often, the shortcoming doing most of this dirty work developed in response to the same unhealed wounds and deep emotions that gave rise to her goal.

"Always look to the character's dark side," says author Chelsea Quinn Yarbro. "There's more material there."

Conflict Equals Suspense

Every story is a suspense story.

That doesn't necessarily mean Suspense with a capital S— the edge-of-the-seat, nail-biting, adrenaline-surging kind. Sometimes it is a tension that hums beneath the surface of the action. But every story should generate in its readers a sense of anticipation, a mix of hope and doubt: What happens next? How will this all turn out?

Suspense is conflict's twin, or perhaps its shadow. If you set up a provocative conflict and play it out carefully, suspense marches along right beside it. Suspense grows out of your readers' desire to have the protagonist achieve her goal and their uncertainty about if and how the conflict will be resolved.

Creating suspense involves drawing your readers in and then keeping them hanging. A writer I know who is also an amateur magician likens writing fiction to performing magic tricks: "Stage magicians have a saying about how to handle an audience: First you make them care, then you make them wait. With stories it's the same thing." The interval between engaging the readers and letting them learn your character's fate is where suspense comes in.

The more uncertainty readers feel, the greater the suspense. If you'd like to ratchet it up a few notches, here are some time-honored techniques:

1. RAISE THE STAKES.

Every time you get your main character in worse trouble, up the ante for her. Make the consequences of success or failure more dire.

Remember to keep the risk and the payoff in balance. If you raise the risk that she confronts, you must also increase the benefit that comes if she succeeds. Otherwise, if she has any sense at all, your protagonist will cut her losses and walk out of the story.

2. ELIMINATE THE OPTIONS.

Keep reducing the number of solutions that remain available to your character. As she tries each one, have it fail for some reason, until with the last possibility she finally succeeds (or does she?). Suspense is built when you lead the characters—and readers—to believe a solution will work, then shut it off at the last minute.

3. ISOLATE YOUR CHARACTER.

Isolate your character physically. Put her in a tight spot, literally, confined to a small space or a locked place, or one that for some reason she can't easily leave. Send her far away from where she wants or needs to be, to an unfamiliar place where she has no knowledge of how to tap into whatever resources might be available for help.

Another option is to isolate her psychologically and emotionally. Send her to a place where she doesn't speak the language or for some other reason can't make herself understood. Create a situation in which no one believes her, no one is willing to help. Place her among people she cannot trust.

When you box in a character like this, you tap into basic fears that the reader shares, like claustrophobia and the fear of being abandoned or deserted.

4. IGNITE A TICKING BOMB.

Set your character in a race against the clock. Not only must she solve the problem and overcome an obstacle to achieve her goal, she must do it within a certain time frame—with serious consequences if she fails to meet the deadline.

In action movies, the ticking bomb is frequently an actual explosive device. Sometimes the villains kindly provide a digital readout, pressuring the heroes by letting them count down the minutes until the device detonates. Your "bomb" doesn't have to be destructive in this literal way. The protagonist's deadline could be the starting time of the meeting that will be crucial to her career, or the day of her wedding, or the night of the high school reunion, or the moment when the airplane arrives with her daughter on board.

To make things even more harrowing, keep your protagonist from knowing exactly when the deadline is. The detective must find the murderer before he strikes again—but will that be next week, or in the next hour?

Exercises: Finding Story Conflict

1. Choose three short stories to read and think about. For each story, write brief answers to the following questions:

   a. What is the protagonist's main goal or desire in this story? How does it change as the story proceeds?

   b. What is the central conflict in this story? Who or what is the antagonist or main opposing force?

   c. What obstacles or problems does the protagonist encounter in trying to resolve the conflict and reach the goal? What sources of conflict does the author draw upon to create these obstacles?

   d. How do the protagonist's strengths or weaknesses influence the progress of the story?

   e. When do we first become aware of the existence of conflict or tension?

   f. What does the author do to generate suspense?

2. Read *The Life of the Party* on page 53. Pick two of the characters—a protagonist and an antagonist—and write a scene that brings out the conflict between them. Feel free to add details; you don't need to stick to the events described. Use these questions as a guideline:

   a. What does the protagonist want? What is his or her goal or desire?

   b. What does the antagonist want?

   c. Where do these goals conflict?

   d. What other sources of conflict could be here?

   e. Where is the party, and why is it being held?

   f. What events occurred before this scene and led up to it?

   g. What will happen next?

3. Select a letter from Dear Abby, Ann Landers, or a similar newspaper advice column. Based on the situation described in the letter, select a protagonist and an antagonist and write a scene that brings out the conflict. Use the questions in

Exercise 2 as a guideline. Feel free to add details; you need not stick to the events described in the letter or pay attention to the columnist's counsel.

4. Rewrite one of the scenes you created to heighten the suspense to the greatest degree you can.

5. Pretend that you are the protagonist of a suspense story (Suspense with a capital S) and you have landed in one of the dilemmas below. Write a scene describing the situation, making it as dire and suspenseful as possible. Be inventive, and be sure to explain how you get out of the jam.

   ■ The villain has taken you to a remote cabin in the mountains. You are locked inside, and the doors and windows are blocked. You are miles from the nearest town. There is no telephone. A blizzard has buried all the roads and trails deep in snow. You do not know the territory. The villain has told you that he or she will come back in the evening to kill you.

   ■ You and your friend have been locked by the villain in an abandoned warehouse. As you were exploring, trying to find a way out, your friend fell from a ledge and broke his/her leg. Now you realize that the villain has set the warehouse on fire. You must get yourself and your friend out quickly.

   ■ You have sneaked into the villain's office late at night when no one is there in order to find the evidence to prove that she/he has committed the crime you are investigating. While you are searching the office, which is on the 27th floor of the building, you hear a noise. You realize that the villain has arrived unexpectedly and is about to come in the room and discover you. You are unarmed, but she or he is probably carrying a gun.

Chapter 4

Plot and Structure

*How to Shape Your Story
and Keep It Moving Forward*

Characters in one hand, a conflict in the other—this is the point where you begin structuring a story.

The story's structure is its organizational system, the means by which you establish the relationships of its various elements and bind them into a coherent whole. The structure gives the story its shape in the same way that a framework gives shape to a house.

Most of the time in fiction, structure equates with plot. Although there are other ways to structure a story, a plot is the most common, the most traditional and the most versatile. A plot is what a child wants to hear when, bright-eyed and eager, she begs, "Tell me a story."

What Is a Plot?

Plot is a concept that perplexes a lot of us—nonwriters, new writers, and old pros.

If "Where do you get your ideas?" is the question most frequently asked of writers, the silver medal winner must be: "How do you think up your plots?"

One correct answer is: "One step at a time." An equally accurate response is: "I don't—I let the characters do it for me." You construct a plot bit by bit, by listening to your characters, testing ideas on them, and seeing which ones make them spring to life.

Of all the essential ingredients of a story, plot is perhaps the hardest to grasp. It does not lend itself to easy definitions. The word *plot* is both verb and noun. It means the process by which you build an idea into a story (*I can't go to the movies tonight; I have to buckle down and plot out the short story I'm writing for class*) and it also refers to the structure that results.

PLOT VERSUS PREMISE

"Oh, you're writing a story," your friend says to you. "What's the plot?" What he's really asking for is the premise. It's easy to get the two concepts confused.

In logic or debate, a premise is an assertion that serves as the basis for an argument or for a particular line of reasoning. In fiction writing, think of it as the dramatic situation at the heart of the story, which can be summarized in a line or two. You'll find premises in the log lines in *TV Guide* and the blurbs in the best-seller list or the book review column: the line or two that reports what the program or book is about. The premise is the cocktail party description, the twenty-five-words-or-less you use in casual conversation, intriguing enough to make people want to read the story yet short enough to keep their eyes from glazing over with boredom. In Hollywood, when moviemakers speak of *high concept*—a bold, exciting storyline that can be encapsulated in a single sentence—they are referring to a premise.

A plot is something much greater. The plot is what happens in the story, all of its events and actions. To tell your friend the plot, you would have to outline the entire narrative.

PLOTS AND PLANS

One dictionary defines *plot* as "a series of dramatic events moving forward in time." This is true, but as we'll see, it is only part of the picture—a necessary component, but not sufficient to define a plot.

Take Wednesday morning for example. Your alarm fails to go off, so you awaken late. Getting ready for work, you drop the soap in the shower and slip on it, slamming your knee against the tiles. Your spouse picks an argument with you over breakfast. As you're driving through the commuter traffic, the car in front of you stops suddenly, forcing you to crunch its bumper.

When you limp into the office, your boss announces that the firm has just lost its biggest account. Several employees, you among them, are being laid off.

On this miserable day, you are smack up against dramatic events, and you have plenty of conflict. But you don't have a plot.

Another definition calls a plot "a story's plan of action." By introducing the notion of planning, this moves us a step closer to understanding plot, both the noun and the verb. After all, the words *plot* and *plan* are cousins, close to being synonyms.

In Chapter One we noted that, in fiction, events have a purpose. They are hooked to each other like jigsaw puzzle pieces or connect-the-dots lines to carry out the author's intended design. To construct a plot, you make conscious decisions about which of your characters' actions, thoughts, and circumstances are important to tell, and which you should leave out. You choose the ones that will contribute to your story goal, lead to resolution or closure, and reinforce the story's theme, mood, and emotional and dramatic impact.

How do you go about planning, or plotting, your story? That's up to you.

Some authors do extensive preparatory work. They scribble reams of notes, make charts, construct biographies of characters, devise outlines, and lay out a detailed blueprint for the story to come. Only when they think they know the story thoroughly, beginning to end, do they actually start to write it.

Others plunge right into the first draft, hoping to discover the story as it unfolds on the page. In the second draft (or the third or the fourth), once the story has revealed itself, they fine-tune it, sharpening the elements that count and ripping out the ones, however beautifully written, that are not earning their keep.

Many writers combine these two techniques, planning a little, then putting the characters through a few paces on the page, then planning some more when the answer to *What happens next?* isn't clear. Often it's helpful when you start writing a story to have at least a vague sense of what the ending will be. That little bit of knowledge serves as a beacon to guide you as you make choices about the story.

Are you a planner or a plunger? Finding the approach that works for you is a matter of trial and error. The creative process works differently for each of us, and every story makes its own demands.

Four Characteristics of a Plot

To pull all this together, let's look more closely at the four qualities that define a plot, that make a sequence of events a story instead of the haphazard occurrences of a frustrating Wednesday morning. They are:

1. A character with a goal and a conflict.

2. Movement forward in time.

3. Causality and connectedness of events.

4. Direction toward an answer or a resolution.

Tuck an awareness of these characteristics into the back of your mind as you read stories and as you devise your own plots. They will help you develop your intuitive sense of how a plot works.

I. A CHARACTER IN CONFLICT

To create a plot, begin with the three questions about the protagonist that we asked in Chapter Three:

1. What does the protagonist want to accomplish or gain in the course of this story?

2. What will be the consequences, to her and to others, if she hits or misses this goal?

3. Who or what gets in her way?

These questions establish the nature of the conflict. The plot is the means by which the conflict is resolved. It describes how the protagonist does (or does not) overcome the obstacles that impede her and how she succeeds (or fails) in achieving her goal.

Which comes first, the plot or the characters? That's a chicken-and-egg question. If you have one without the other, you have no story. The two are so intricately bound together, it's impossible to separate them.

Sometimes your flour idea for a story might be a premise, some sort of dramatic situation or incident. The trick in that case is to find the right characters to adopt that premise as their own. At other times a character marches into your mind and announces he wants to be in a story. Then you must figure out what kind of situation and conflict this person would become involved in, given his particular personality, desires, motives, and circumstances.

Either way, the success of the story depends on your carefully matching the people to the plot. Frequently, what seem to be plotting problems are in fact problems with a character. If you try to force a character to get into a situation that's not right for him, or to act or react in ways he would not naturally do, he's likely to balk, which stalls your writing process; or to become wooden, which makes the story sound contrived or forced.

Veteran authors often say the characters will tell you the story if you sit back and listen. While that can be true, there's more to it than simply taking dictation. You may have to cajole the story out of them, presenting various ideas and asking, "Okay, will this work?" The characters will give you helpful answers if you pay attention.

2. MOVEMENT FORWARD IN TIME

If it's a plot, it's about time.

The dictionary is correct, if incomplete, in calling a plot "a series of dramatic events moving forward in time." The chronological progression of incidents is what gives the story a beginning, a middle, and an end. The plot of a story is everything that occurs between "Once upon a time" and "They lived happily ever after." It answers an important question: "Then what happened?"

How much time is involved depends on the story. A plot can cover a few minutes, an hour, a day, a year, a lifetime, or more. Short stories tend to have short time frames; that way the limited number of words available isn't spread too thinly over too many events. But you can write a perfectly effective story that spans decades.

Although the incidents of a plot parade forward in succession, the story itself might not. In no way are you required to recount the events in consecutive order. For many stories, a straight chronological narrative is the best way to reach your story goal. In other cases, though, simply stringing out the sequence of events could mean shortchanging other demands of the story—the need to elucidate a character, say, or to create a mood, or to set up the desired emotional response in the reader.

The author's task, in other words, is to arrange and present the events in the way that will achieve the greatest dramatic impact. Here are some sample techniques, by no means an exhaustive survey:

■ **Flashbacks.** A flashback occurs any time you interrupt the forward motion to recount an earlier incident that has bearing on the story. By using a flashback, you can drop readers directly into the action of a scene and then step back to let us know how we arrived at this time and place. You can delve deeply into your characters' memories, or bring in background from their histories that helps to illuminate what is happening to them now.

■ **Frames.** With a frame, the opening and closing scenes mirror each other. They occur in the same place or at the same moment in time, so that when readers reach the end, they are reminded of the beginning. The bulk of the story, though, happens at other times or locations. The result is something like a story within a story. You might employ a frame, for example, to allow a character the opportunity to offer a more mature perspective on experiences she had when she was younger. At the start, the older woman introduces herself as a girl and sets up the story; at the end she returns to offer some insight she has gained over time.

Another use of a frame is to set the stage for the resolution of the story by giving us an advance peek at where we are headed. In William Faulkner's *A Rose for Emily*, the story begins and ends as townspeople arrive at Miss Emily Grierson's home for her funeral. Their entrance into the house inspires the nameless narrator to share the history, as far as the town knows it, of this reclusive old spinster, and it prepares the way for their postmortem discovery of Miss Emily's secret.

A frame can facilitate a story's sense of closure. It brings the readers around full circle, so that we return to the point where we started but now view it with a more complete understanding.

- **Multiple views of a single event.** Do you recall John Godfrey Saxe's poem, *The Blind Men and the Elephant*? One of the men had hold of the beast's tusk, another felt its trunk, a third man its leg, and someone else its ear. Each of them, based on his own observation, reached a conclusion about the elephant's true nature—the animal resembled a spear; a snake; a tree; a fan.

In a similar way, any one of your characters has an incomplete and perhaps misleading perspective on what's going on. When you show the same event through more than one viewpoint, you can provide more accurate insight into the nature of your story elephant. Don't do it all at once though; rather than jump from character to character within a single scene to give us everybody's take on things, try replaying the event a couple of times, letting us witness it fully each time through someone else's eyes.

In *The Lilac Bus*, author Maeve Binchy describes the events of a single weekend in eight interconnected short stories, each told from the point of view of a different resident of a small Irish town. All eight characters undergo life-changing events during the course of the forty-eight hours. Although they keep crossing paths with each other, their experiences and perspectives are divergent and highly personal.

- **Layers of time.** For some stories, you may wish to set linear movement aside. Instead, let the events jump around in time in a way that seems almost random. It's not random, of course; what you're really doing is arranging impressions and tidbits of information in the order that will let you build most compellingly to the climax. The best presentation may have nothing to do with the chronological sequence of events. The effect is as if you had taken the fabric of time, folded it into layers, and run the story through the layers like a needle.

3. CAUSALITY AND CONNECTEDNESS

When I taught writing to fourth graders, the first stories they wrote came straight from the videogame arcade. There was plenty of conflict; no sooner would the hero blast away one enemy than a new one would pop up in front of the castle gates or zoom down from the Planet Xorg. But there was no plot. The monsters or space aliens were never in cahoots with one another; there was no cause-and-effect connection between the new problem and the previous one. With no way to provide a satisfying conclusion, the young author would simply run out of steam and declare the story over.

If your protagonist wanders aimlessly about, slaying random dragons, you have no plot. The characters bear some responsibility for assembling their various activities, however disconnected they may seem, into a cohesive story.

Almost all fiction, at its heart, explores some aspect of the same topic: the choices people make and the ramifications of those choices. Faced with a situation, a person chooses how he will respond to it—whether to move forward or backward, to resist or give in, to take a risk or avoid one. This decision sets up a new situation, one that might or might not be in accord with what the chooser hoped or intended. Another response, another choice, is now required.

A plot, then, in its simplest form, is a chain of causes and effects, of choices and their repercussions, as pictured in this simple graph.

Action → Consequence → Action → Consequence

The characters' choices are expressed in their actions. Each action leads to consequences, and each consequence generates the next action: Because this happened, then that happened as a result.

Writer Janet Dawson calls this the domino theory of plotting. If you stand dominoes on end, set them in a row, and push the first one over, they will all tumble in sequence if they have been lined up correctly. Similarly, when you set a plot in motion with a particular incident, that event triggers the next one, and the next, and the subsequent incidents will inevitably follow.

Here's an example of how actions and consequences work in, well, action:

...Because Molly's alarm didn't go off, she was late for school...

...Because she was late, she was rushing down the sidewalk...

...Because she was rushing down the sidewalk, she collided with Veronica...

...Because Molly collided with Veronica, Veronica fell off the curb and badly bruised her knee...

...Because Molly made Veronica hurt her knee, she felt guilty...

...Because she felt guilty about hurting Veronica, Molly decided she should say yes when Veronica asked to copy her answers on the science quiz, even though Molly knew it was wrong and cheating made her feel uncomfortable...

...Because Molly felt uncomfortable, she acted nervous and fidgety during the quiz...

...Because she was nervous and fidgety, the teacher became suspicious and caught Molly and Veronica cheating...

...Because Molly and Veronica got in trouble for cheating....

What happens next? Based on this set of incidents, you can construct a story, or several stories. Molly, Veronica, and the teacher have individual personalities, and they react to events in their own ways. Each has her personal goals and desires, which will be affected by this incident's outcome. Change any detail, and the story will change. Are Molly and Veronica seven years old, or seventeen? Until now, have they been friends or rivals? Does Veronica habitually cheat, or was she yielding to a one-time temptation? Is the teacher kindly or mean? Has a recent scandal caused the school to crack down on students who cheat?

The story will also change if Molly or Veronica chooses a different response to what has happened. Suppose, for instance, that Molly said no when Veronica asked to copy her quiz answers. Would that have ended the matter, or would Veronica have demanded a different favor or chosen another way to get even?

Having a chain of actions and consequences means that you can't toss in handy coincidences to force the story to move in a particular direction. Nor can you fly in a *deus ex machina* to come to your protagonist's rescue. This Latin term means "god from a machine." Originally it referred to a custom in classical theater: At a crucial point in the action, a god would be trundled in on creaky stage machinery to intervene in the mortals' lives. The phrase has come to mean any trick, improbable device, or twist of fate that an author employs to arbitrarily change a character's fortunes.

Playing the "what if..." game can help you work through the procession of actions and consequences. What if this happens—how would this character, or that one, respond? Suppose she chooses to take this action—what would be the likely result? And so on down the chain.

Of course, a story is seldom so straightforward. Events can occur that are beyond a character's instigation or control. Other characters' actions can impinge on her; the weather may ruin her plans; a declaration of war may throw her life into upheaval. All of these occurrences will demand that she do something in response. A single story may involve several chains of actions and consequences, which the author weaves together in a web.

Among all the options that present themselves, how do you decide which incidents and details to include and which to leave out? The ones that belong are those that connect to your story goal and to the central issue you are using the story to explore. That brings us to the fourth characteristic of a plot.

4. DIRECTION TOWARD AN ANSWER OR A RESOLUTION

A short story answers a question—several questions, in fact. You set them up at the beginning to engage the readers' interest. The story itself is your promise that they will be answered, and the plot is the means by which the promise is fulfilled.

The first question is the most obvious: Will the protagonist get what she wants? You may bring in other questions as well, especially if the story concerns some sort of secret: Who done it? What's in the box? Where did the stranger come from?

There is another question, too, that is both larger and more subtle than these, the one that expresses the central issue of the story. This is the one that you as the author pose for yourself, whether consciously or unconsciously, as you sit down to write; the one you are writing the story to discover.

The central issue might double as the protagonist's goal, but it does not necessarily have to. In Charles Dickens' *A Christmas Carol*, Ebenezer Scrooge's goals are to keep making money at his business, to avoid disruptions in what he has convinced himself is a comfortable life, and, as the story progresses, to deal with those annoying ghosts. The central issue is more significant: Will Scrooge turn into a human being and come to realize the value of human connections and relationships?

The sense of closure that readers experience at the end of the story comes from having the central issue and its related questions resolved. This resolution is the destination the story must reach. All of the story elements function as signposts pointing both writer and readers in that direction.

It's not necessary to identify the central issue or to have any answers before you begin. Writing is a process of discovering the questions as much as it is about finding the answers, and that's a great part of its joy. But if a story is being elusive, try defining the central issue. That may be one way to grasp hold of it and push it forward.

Building the Narrative Structure

By now you have assembled a number of questions, a handful of answers, some ideas about conflict, and a few characters whom you're beginning to know. You're eager to start putting everything down on the page. How do you take these bits and pieces, these threads and snippets, and fabricate them into a story?

THE FIVE CLASSIC PARTS

Just as buildings, from sheds to skyscrapers, have certain parts in common—floors, walls, roofs—so do stories. Since classical times, writers have constructed stories using the same five basic parts. The diagram on page 81 provides a rough generic blueprint of a plot. The thick line represents the course of a story, showing how it progresses from beginning to end.

In architecture, a given part can take numerous forms. Think of the many available options for windows, from tiny leaded diamond panes to vast expanses of plate glass. A roof can be flat or steeply pitched, and covered with shingles or slates or thick grass thatch. The number, arrangement, and individual style of the parts are what give the building its distinctive character. In a similar way, the parts of a story lend themselves to infinite variation. The five parts are:

■ **Inciting incident.** This is also sometimes called the exciting force. Whether inciting or exciting, it's what starts the ball rolling—the event that begins or intensifies the protagonist's predicament. This action sets up a situation that will need to be resolved and creates the opportunity for the conflict to occur.

■ **Complications.** This is how you get your protagonist in trouble and worse trouble. Complications are the obstacles the protagonist faces, the turns of events that make reaching her goal more difficult. Remember that complications can spring from the characters' own actions—for instance, when they choose unwisely or when the results of their choices don't turn out as planned.

Complications arise throughout the story, up to the moment of climax. Notice that the line on the diagram rises for most of its length; this signifies the heightening of tension as the story proceeds and the complications accumulate.

■ **Crisis.** We think of a crisis as being some sort of emergency, one that is likely to have a disastrous outcome if we don't take action quickly. That's not exactly the meaning in terms of story structure. In literature, a crisis is a decisive moment or event, a turning point. The Greek root, *krisis*, means "to separate"; the crisis separates what has gone before from what comes afterward. Often it marks a change, at least temporarily, in the fortunes of one or more characters. In screenwriting, the crisis is called a plot point—the point on which a story pivots as it spins in a new direction—which is perhaps a more helpful way to describe it.

A novel may have several major and minor plot points. A short story, though, generally has room for only one or two. In some stories the crisis and climax may be almost simultaneous.

■ **Climax.** We have now reached the culminating event in our series of actions. On the diagram the rising line has reached its peak. The Greek word *klimax* means "ladder," and the story has been climbing to the point of its highest excitement and power—the confrontation between protagonist and antagonist. This is the moment when the hero's success or failure is determined once and for all. In the climax, the conflict is resolved and the answers to the principal questions raised by the story become clear.

■ **Denouement.** This word is borrowed from the French; the root is *denouer*, "to untie." To the ancients, a story was a knot; its resolution meant that the knot was finally unraveled and whatever secrets or misunderstandings had been bound up in it were at last revealed. It is just as useful to reverse the metaphor; think of the denouement as the time to tie up loose ends and conclude the action.

As you can see on the diagram, the tension is finally falling. In today's literature, the tendency is to push the climax as close as possible to the end of story, then wrap things up quickly so as not to diminish the impact.

NARRATIVE STRUCTURE

2. Complications

4. Climax, or Confrontation

1. Inciting Incident

3. Crises, or Plot Point

5. Denouement or Resolution

A PUMPKIN COACH AND A GLASS SLIPPER

To get a better idea of how narrative structure works, let's apply it to a familiar tale—a Disneyesque version of *Cinderella*.

You remember Cindy. She's the sad drudge who is forced by her evil stepsisters to dress in rags and do the household scut work while they preen in silken finery and indulge themselves in pleasures. The central issue of the story is: Will Cinderella break away from the family's clutches and find happiness?

The inciting incident occurs when the household receives an invitation to a ball at the royal palace. The stepsisters are atwitter with excitement, and not only at the prospect of enjoying all that glitter and glamour. Here is their chance to beguile the Prince with their beauty, perhaps even to snag him as a husband for one stepsister or the other.

Cindy, of course, would like to go to the ball also. This is her desire as the tale begins. But if she were simply to attend the party with the others, there would be no story. Happily, her relatives create complications. They forbid her to go. They make her help stitch up their gorgeous gowns while they mock her dowdy work dress. They set her to sweeping ashes out of the hearth while they dress for an evening of dancing. Finally they step into their fine coach and ride off, leaving a tearful Cindy behind. End of story.

Hold on...it's not the end after all. Here we have the first crisis, a moment at which the story heads in a new direction. The fairy godmother appears.

This is the answer Cinderella has been hoping for. The fairy godmother, a resourceful type, restyles Cindy's rags into a gown of gold and gossamer, converts a pumpkin from the garden into a coach, and changes the house mice into high-stepping horses to pull it. When Cindy arrives at the palace, the Prince is enchanted by the beauty she has finally revealed. He falls madly in love with this mysterious, unknown woman—surely a princess—and decides he must marry her. End of story.

Except...there are further complications. The magic that transformed Cinderella came with strings attached. At the stroke of midnight, everything will revert to its original state—coach to pumpkin, horses to mice, ball gown to tattered dress, and Cinderella to, well, Cinderella again. But Cindy—enjoying the festivities, thrilled by the attentions of the Prince, smugly satisfied by her stepsisters' envy and dismay—loses track of the time.

When the clock strikes twelve Cindy panics and flees, leaving the bewildered Prince behind. The magic ends, and her life returns to the way it was before the fairy godmother appeared. End of story.

But wait...we have another crisis, a second turning point. As Cinderella dashes away from the ball, one of her glass slippers falls from her foot. The Prince finds it on the palace steps and sets out on a quest, determined to have every young woman in the land try it on. He will marry the one whose foot fits the tiny, delicate shoe, for she must be his beloved, mysterious princess.

Naturally his search leads him to Cinderella's house, where the evil stepsisters have been working poor Cindy harder than ever. The moment of confrontation and climax is at hand.

The stepsisters, thrilled by the Prince's arrival, are determined to cram their feet into the slipper. Alas, try as they might, their feet are too big. (An early version of this tale has them chopping off their own toes in an effort to make the shoe fit.) The Prince is about to leave the house in despair when he spots Cindy with her tattered dress and old broom. Despite the stepsisters' protests, he invites her to try on the glass slipper. Of course it slides easily onto her foot.

Finally we have the denouement. The stepsisters, with their greed and ambition and cruelty, are vanquished. Arm in arm with her Prince, Cinderella returns in triumph to the palace, where they live happily ever after.

Beginnings, Middles, and Ends

Notice that in *Cinderella* there are two turning points or moments of crisis. In effect, they divide the story into three acts:

Act One is **the setup**, in which the stepsisters' cruelty to Cinderella is established and we see the preparations for the ball. This act includes the inciting incident and the first complication, and ends with a turning point—the arrival of the fairy godmother.

Act Two is **the development**, in which the fairy godmother performs her magic and, under its spell, Cinderella goes to the ball and charms the Prince. This act ends when the clock strikes twelve, the magic dissolves, and Cinderella loses the precious glass slipper.

Act Three is **the resolution**, in which the Prince searches out his mysterious princess, the stepsisters get their comeuppance, and Cinderella prevails.

In other words, we have a beginning, a middle, and an end.

The screenplay is a storytelling form with rules as rigid as those of a sonnet in poetry. It follows a strict three-act structure.

Each act is a prescribed length, with Act One taking up the first quarter of the picture's running time, Act Two occupying the middle half, and Act Three playing out in the final quarter. At the end of each of the first two acts, a major plot point occurs to launch the events of the act that follows.

An entertaining way to teach yourself about story structure is to watch movies with the three acts in mind. See if you can identify the major plot points and discern where the different acts begin and end. This can be hard to do on a first viewing because you're caught up by the characters and their problems. But if you watch the film a second or third time, when you already know how the story turns out, the pattern of acts will become more clear.

A good film for this exercise is *Witness*, starring Harrison Ford and Kelly McGillis, because its three acts are delineated clearly and distinctly. An Amish boy, traveling with his widowed mother, witnesses a murder in a Philadelphia train station. The cop who questions the pair discovers that other police officers are involved in the crime. As he investigates, he is shot and wounded. Fearing that the woman and child are in danger, he hides their identities from his fellow cops and drives them back to their farm. Then, weakened by his injury, he crashes his car as he leaves; this is the plot point that ends Act One. In Act Two the cop, hiding from colleagues who want to kill him, recuperates at the woman's home. This act focuses on the relationship between the cop and the young widow, the clash of their cultures and their growing attraction to each other. Then comes a second plot point: An incident occurs that causes someone to report the man's whereabouts to the police. In Act Three, the villains arrive at the farm. A cat-and-mouse game ensues, culminating in the confrontation between the good and evil officers of the law.

In fiction, the three acts are usually less formal and obvious. In fact, quite likely they aren't present at all; a novelist or short story writer need not adhere to the kind of formal structure required of a screenwriter. Authors with a finely tuned story sense may use this structure instinctively without even being conscious of it.

You might find it helpful to think in terms of the three acts as you begin to conceptualize and organize the action of your story: What belongs at the beginning, what happens in the middle, and how should it end? Let's take a closer look at these issues.

THE BEGINNING: PULLING THE READER IN

You have a big job to do in Act One. You must grab our attention, set up the story, and ignite our desire to read through to the end. Here's how you accomplish this:

■ **Start with a strong narrative hook.** Like the hook on a line that snags fish, a narrative hook catches readers. It lets you grab our attention and reel us into your story. Compare these two possible openings:

Version 1: Once there lived a woman named Cinderella. She was beautiful but sad. Her two stepsisters were mean and evil. They always treated her cruelly. They made her dress in rags and do all the household chores.

Then one day a messenger arrived. He brought an invitation to a ball at the royal palace.

Version 2: How beautiful, Cinderella marveled. What could this be? The messenger at her door extended his silver tray with the missive resting upon it. The folded parchment was of the finest quality and the wax that sealed it was golden. Impressed into the wax was the King's coat of arms.

But Cinderella didn't dare pick it up. Even though she had brushed her fingers against her tattered skirt, they were covered with soot.

"Cinderella!" shrieked her stepsister, the older one with the drab brown hair. "Whatever made you think you were allowed to answer the door? Back to the scullery, you worthless girl, there's work to be done."

In the second version, readers stand at the doorstep with Cinderella, sharing her awe and curiosity regarding the message on the silver tray. We feel her humiliation when the screeching stepsister arrives. Instead of simply being told the stepsister is cruel, we experience it firsthand. We want to know more about the conflict we already see brewing. If readers never get past the first paragraphs, all the art and craft you've put into the story will be for naught. Once upon a time, a writer could be leisurely in introducing a story, but times and styles have changed. People today lead busy, fast-paced lives. We have competing demands for our attention and plenty of entertainment options to choose from. We give you a moment or two to sell us on reading your story, and if we aren't intrigued we'll quickly move on to something else.

Start your story in a way that will compel our interest and suggest the conflict to come. If you are quick to arouse our curiosity and involve us in the action, we're sure to keep reading.

■ **Jump into the action.** Don't feel you must explain everything—who, what, when, where, why—in the first paragraphs. We will want to know these things fairly soon, but as we watch and listen to the characters, we'll enjoy the pleasure of discovering them for ourselves. If you must explain something, weave the explanation into the action—let one character tell another, or show us through the viewpoint character's thoughts or observations. This is the opening of my story, *The Old Furiosity Shoppe*:

> The plate soared in a high arc, the face on it wild-eyed, grimacing. Then it hit the brick wall and shattered, the fragments tumbling to the floor. Isaac smiled as he swept them up. He could make out a corner of the mouth, an eyelid, a bit of nostril.
>
> "Aw right!" whooped the kid who had sailed the plate. He raised his fist in triumph as his buddies applauded.
>
> "Way to go, Danny!" yelled the redhead. "That sure takes care of ol' man Cuthbert."
>
> "I wanna do one," said the reedy boy with the ghost of a mustache.
>
> "Griswold this time," Danny decided. "The creep flunked me on that stupid math test."
>
> The boys pushed dollar bills at Isaac, who stuffed the money in the cashbox and handed out clean white plates and marking pens. The kids set to work sketching the faces of their enemies on the crockery.

The strong but perplexing image in the first paragraph becomes clear as we come to realize, without being told, that we are in a business establishment. At the Old Furiosity

Shoppe, customers pay to vent their frustrations by drawing them on crockery which they then smash.

■ **Introduce the important characters.** As much as possible, let us see them in action. Make it clear who the protagonist is, and let her begin to win our interest and sympathy. If a character who plays a key role won't show up until later in the story, introduce him in absentia, through the conversation of the characters who are present or by some other means. In *Cinderella*, the Prince doesn't come on stage until midway through Act Two, but the stepsisters, by their excited reaction to the invitation to the ball, tell us right away that he's important to the story.

■ **Present the inciting incident.** This moment may take place on- or off-stage, but it should occur early in the story. In fact, it might have transpired even before the story opens. If so, depict it in a flashback or discuss it in dialogue so that readers clearly understand what it is.

■ **Set up the questions and conflicts.** By the end of Act One, we should have a sense of what's at stake—the central issue of the story, the protagonist's predicament and her goal, and the principal conflict to be resolved. The tension should be buzzing from the outset; remember, there is no flat place on the story line on the narrative structure diagram.

■ **Wrap up this section with the first plot point or crisis.** Choose a significant complication to create the forward movement that propels us into the middle of the story.

THE MIDDLE: KEEPING UP THE MOMENTUM

The middle, Act Two, is the longest section of your story. Your task is to make sure the story keeps rolling and the readers keep reading. In writing the middle you have four objectives:

■ **Develop the characters and their relationships.** As the story proceeds, we should come to know them better and better—their personalities, their motives, the basis for the kinds of choices they make.

■ **Prevent them from reaching their goals.** In Act Two the characters are attempting to straighten out their conflicts and predicaments. Attempting is the key word; don't make it too easy for them. Although you will have introduced some complications in Act One and you'll have important ones coming up in Act Three's dash to the climax, the bulk of the barriers and obstacles come in this section.

■ **Keep the tension rising.** Make sure that as the complications progress, the stakes to be settled in the confrontation become ever higher and the outcome increasingly in doubt.

■ **Set up the finale with a new plot point or crisis.** Another significant complication as Act Two winds up will propel us into the endgame of the story.

The middle is where stories, and their authors, are likely to bog down. Often a writer knows in the early stages how a story will start and finish, but the middle—that vast gap to be bridged between the beginning and the end—remains obscured in fog. Too often, stories sputter to a halt after a few promising pages, and wind up in the back of a desk drawer, never to be completed.

To keep yourself on course, bear in mind that a story's purpose is to provide answers to a series of questions—the central issue plus the three key questions that provide your characters' motivation. When the story starts to move in the wrong direction, it's often because the author has lost sight of those questions or never figured them out in the first place.

Other sources of difficulties in the middle are:

■ Not having a strong enough sense of who your characters are, what they want, and what they would do in a given situation.

■ Trying to force actions on your characters or manipulate them into doing things that are contrary to their own natures or circumstances.

■ Including actions in the story that don't arise as a result of previous actions. Don't forget, when characters make choices, consequences ensue; how they respond to those consequences determines the next action. If you follow that cause-and-effect chain, it often leads you directly to the story's end.

■ Letting the tension flag. This happens for two main reasons. First, it may be that risk and payoff are out of balance. Perhaps the complications the protagonist faces do not pose an increasing degree of threat to her goal; we never doubt that she will achieve it. Conversely, the complications may have become so great that achieving the goal is no longer worth the risk. Either way, the outcome is no longer sufficiently in doubt. Second, the writer may be interrupting his own story by digressing into side discussions, inserting unnecessary scenes, or injecting authorial asides that pull readers out of the story world.

■ Sidestepping the conflicts. Yes, conflicts can be unpleasant. But you must allow the characters to grapple with the forces that oppose them, even if doing so causes them (and you) some pain. A big reason that stories don't succeed is because their authors set up significant issues and then pull away from dealing with them. Writing any story is an act of courage; it pays to let yourself muster enough bravery to carry it through all the way.

Remember, the story belongs to the characters. The struggles and choices are theirs. The course the story takes and the resolution it finally reaches may not be at all what you expected when you started writing.

If you need help in figuring out what happens next, ask your characters and see what they say. Here's a technique that may prove worthwhile: At the top of a page (either on paper or on a computer screen) write a direct question, addressing the character by name:

Alex, what are you going to do next?

Isabel, what do you want to get out of this situation?

Eric, you seem angry. What are you angry about?

Mrs. Featherstone, what are you doing in this story anyway?

Now, let them answer. Start writing, using the character's voice in the first person, stream-of-consciousness style. Don't stop to think; don't lift your pen from the paper or your fingers from the keyboard. Just let the words flow, capturing every thought as it comes. Don't edit or go back to correct a misspelling or fix a comma or change a word. After all, this is not material that will appear in your story. It's simply a way of opening a conversation with your subconscious mind so that it can give you the information you need to move forward. Doing this may feel awkward at first, but with a little practice and willingness to let go, it can be a helpful method for tapping into your own creativity. You may be amazed at what your characters are willing to tell you.

Another technique is the "what if..." game described in Chapter One. Don't reserve it for generating story ideas; it's useful at any point in the creative process. By the time you reach the middle of your story, you should know your characters well. As you come up with possible scenarios, you'll be able to sense them shaking their heads sadly over those that won't work, and cheering when you hit on the one they've had in mind all along.

THE END: PROVIDING A STRONG, SATISFYING FINISH

In the final section of your story, Act Three, the action marches inexorably toward the climax. You have turned the last corner. The final complications are those that directly bring about the confrontation between the protagonist and the main opposing force.

This showdown is the moment you have been building up to, the one that rewards your readers for sticking it out until the end. At last we learn the answers to the questions and discover whether the protagonist succeeds or fails.

These pointers will help you bring the story to a satisfying conclusion:

■ **Bring the confrontation to front and center.** This should be the most forceful event in the story, the point of its greatest power and emotion. You can't get away with avoiding it, or soft-pedaling it, or pushing it off-stage.

For maximum impact, place the climax as late in the story as possible. You may need a paragraph or a page for the denouement, where you sort out the remaining strands of your story and bring the action to an end; but try to avoid lengthy or tedious explanations that will dilute the effect of the climax. If many things must be explained, work in the answers to lesser questions before the climax occurs.

■ **Provide an ending worthy of the beginning.** Have you ever had the experience of reading a story that is truly enjoyable for ninety percent of the way, only to have the ending fall flat? This can happen when an author hasn't fully worked out the logical implications of the characters' choices and actions. Many writers like to have at least a vague idea of the ending before they start writing just to avoid this problem. In fact, one practical way to design a plot is to first figure out the finale and then work out the chain of cause and effect backward from there.

If you've laid the proper groundwork for the ending earlier in the story, you won't find yourself relying on tired devices, coincidences, or cop-outs. There will be no need to introduce a character on the last page whose sudden and unexpected appearance somehow explains everything, nor to have your final line read: "She woke up in the morning and realized it was all a dream."

Another reason an ending may fail to satisfy is that the author is trying to spare the characters some hurt, this time the anguish of confrontation. Remember, you cannot protect your characters—the words *protagonist* and *antagonist* have agony built in.

■ **Don't be in a hurry to finish writing.** It's exciting to get close to the end, and after all your hard work, you're naturally eager to bask in the pleasure of accomplishment. The urge to rush—to take shortcuts and make compromises—is almost irresistible. If you give in, the ending is likely to suffer for it. Let the reader be the one who rushes to the end, eager to discover how it all turns out.

Once you have resolved the conflict and answered the questions you've raised, the story is over. You've kept your promise, giving readers a satisfying sense of closure. Having brought this set of circumstances to a reasonable conclusion, you can leave behind some ambiguities and uncertainties about what's in store for the characters. Do Cinderella and the Prince really live happily ever after? That's another story.

Scenes: The Building Blocks of a Plot

The building blocks you use to construct the story—or, if you prefer, the individual dominoes or the links in the chain—are scenes.

A scene is a unit of story action. At a particular time and in a specific place, something happens that is significant to the plot. For instance:

■ A character is introduced or has new light shed upon him.

■ The nature of the relationship between two characters is established.

■ An event takes place—an action, a consequence, a complication—that moves the story forward.

■ A piece of crucial information is provided.

A scene is a small story of its own, a mini-drama with a beginning, a middle, a high point or climactic moment, and an end. A bit of the conflict is played out, and the tension rises.

Depending on the job it needs to do, a scene might be only a few lines long or might continue for several pages; some stories consist of a single extended scene. The second scene in my short story, *Dreaming of Dragons*, comprises the four paragraphs you read on page 24. This scene establishes the story's setting as Chinatown in February when the New Year celebration occurs, introduces the theme of wisdom versus luck, and gives readers their first glimpse at the statue of Buddha, which will be an ongoing motif.

Suppose you were writing *Cinderella* and chose to bring readers into the bedroom as the stepsisters dress for the ball. Such a scene could serve several purposes. For example, as we watch them primp and listen to them chatter, we could discover that the stepsisters are vain, self-centered, and cruel; find out if the pair are rivals or friends; and learn how badly they want to captivate the Prince.

Writing a short story can seem like a formidable project. One way to tackle it and make it more manageable is to break it down into several smaller tasks, by writing scenes. Keep the following points in mind as you do:

- **Create a picture for your readers.** A scene can be visualized, which is what makes it such a powerful means of telling a story. Not only can we see what's happening on the screen of our minds, if you give us the right sensory details we can hear it, smell it, touch it, and taste it as well. Take full advantage of the opportunity to increase your readers' level of involvement.

- **Set the stage quickly.** Three key elements of a scene are time, location, and participating characters. Let us know right away: Where are we, and when? Who is here with us? If we start with an accurate mental picture, we can follow the action easily, even when you choose to be mysterious about exactly what's going on and why. If we realize halfway through the scene that our mental image is wrong, we end up feeling distracted and confused.

- **Make it active.** Action and dialogue are the other two key elements of a scene. Rather than rely on long explanations, let the characters convey information to readers directly through what they say, think, and do.

- **Stick to the point.** Decide what you want to accomplish in the scene, focus the action on that result, and end it quickly.

- **Make a smooth transition to the next scene.** There are a couple of ways to do this, depending on the kind of rhythm and flow you want the story to have. The first is the line break; when you finish Scene One, skip a line and jump straight into Scene Two. The effect is similar to the cuts between scenes in a film. The second way is to include a line or two that covers the shift in place and time:

"Forget it, Josh. It's over. There's nothing more to say." Lisa shut the door. The click of the latch boomed in his ears as if she had slammed it.

Josh rang the doorbell and waited. The curtain flickered in the window that looked out on the porch, and he thought she might be watching him through the pattern of the lace, but he couldn't be sure.

He didn't sleep that night, but lay awake practicing what he would say to her at work the next morning.

"Josh, come here!" Already his boss was yelling and Josh hadn't even had time to hang up his coat.

The line about Josh's failure to sleep is a bridge between the scene just ending at Lisa's front door and the new one just starting at the office the next morning.

Stories without Plots

Not every short story has a plot. Although it would be hard to pull off in a novel, the brevity of a short story allows you to create a strong and satisfying experience for the reader without a plot.

A plotless story can resemble a collection of fragments, like a mosaic, a collage, a quilt, or even a jazz improvisation. At first it may look as though "nothing happens." The images, incidents, and bits of information may seem random, unconnected, or disjointed. Rather than action and character, the author may count on symbols, impressions, rhythms, and the poetic dance of words to create the desired effect, to provide the source of energy that keeps readers involved.

There is still a story goal, a mission the author is trying to accomplish: to evoke an emotion or a mood, to explore a theme, to share an experience, to describe a person, to help the reader comprehend some aspect of the human condition. Each of the fragments contributes to the reader's perception and understanding of this larger whole, so that a sense of unity is achieved at the end. They are not linked by chronology or cause and effect, but by similar emotional or psychological resonances or other things they have in common. Tim O'Brien, in *The Things They Carried*, imparts the experiences of soldiers in Vietnam by cataloging all the various items, and the weight of each, toted by the individual members of an infantry platoon—military gear, personal talismans and treasures, and intangible feelings and fears. Threaded through the inventory is the account of the one soldier's death and the response it invokes in his fellow soldiers and their lieutenant.

Of course, the techniques used to create unplotted stories, such as careful use of language and imagery and thematic links, can be put to excellent purpose in a more traditional narrative. Sometimes, if you dig beneath the surface, a story that appears to have no plot may reveal telltale signs: characters with a conflict to resolve, events that can be listed chronologically, actions that have consequences, and a thrust to a climax and resolution.

Exercises: Constructing a Plot

1. Choose three short stories to read and think about. For each story, write brief answers to the following questions:

   a. What is the organizing principle? Is it plot or something else?

   b. What do you think the central issue of the story is?

   c. What is the inciting incident and at what point in the story does it occur?

   d. What is the protagonist's goal, and what complications interfere with reaching it? Are the sources of the complications internal or external?

   e. Are there plot points or crises that turn the story in a new direction or mark a change in the protagonist's fortunes? What are they?

   f. What event or action constitutes the climax of the story?

   g. Do you feel the story achieves a satisfying resolution? Why or why not?

2. Write the story of Molly and Veronica that begins on page 77. How does the chain of actions and consequences play out? Keep in mind the following questions:

   a. What does Molly want? What does Veronica want?

   b. Where do their goals conflict?

   c. What other sources of conflict might there be?

   d. How do Molly and Veronica feel about what is happening?

   e. What do they do next?

   f. What does the teacher do? What is his or her goal in this story?

   g. Are there other characters involved? For example, other students, the school principal, Molly's or Veronica's parents?

   h. What was the relationship between the two girls at the beginning of the story, and how does it change?

3. Pick a familiar fairy tale (other than *Cinderella*) and:

   a. Depict the story in the form of an actions-and-consequences chain (similar to the one involving Molly and Veronica).

   b. Create a plot outline, indicating what incidents and information will go in the beginning, the middle, and the end.

4. Choose a scene you wrote for one of the exercises in Chapters Two or Three and expand it into a story.

   a. Identify:
      - The goals of the main characters.
      - The conflict.
      - The central issue of the story.

   b. Develop an actions-and-consequences chain.

   c. Create a plot outline, indicating what incidents and information will go in the beginning, the middle, and the end.

Chapter 5

Setting and Atmosphere

How to Bring Readers into a Vivid Story World

Now that your characters are in action, it's time to put them in their place. That place is your story's setting.

Setting does not mean scenery. Far more than just a painted backdrop against which events play out, the setting is a vital force that impinges on the characters and their situations. The setting influences their behavior and provides obstacles that must be overcome. It creates moods and affects emotions for characters and readers alike.

When you write a story you are creating a new world and bidding your readers to enter it. You want us to accept it as true, even when it is jarringly at odds with what we assume about reality. We know Cinderella's kingdom does not exist, but we willingly go there anyway.

The setting establishes the physical and cultural landscape of your invented world. It provides the story's ambiance, the atmosphere that surrounds the characters and readers alike. Rather than a travelogue with long descriptive passages, the setting is most effectively rendered by showing the characters in action within it. Through careful selection of details, you can draw readers directly into the story world, letting us experience it by looking over the characters' shoulders and even through their eyes.

The story world can be modeled on a real place or it can be wholly imagined. It can be restrictive or expansive, small or large: a room, a building, a neighborhood, a city, a region, a planet. Settings are frequently layered, with smaller ones contained within larger ones: We are in this room in this house in this neighborhood in this region, like a set of wooden dolls that nest one inside the other. Each layer contributes to the richness of the fictional environment.

In Eudora Welty's *Death of a Traveling Salesman*, for instance, the salesman is lost on a dead-end country road in the deep South when his car goes into a ditch. He seeks help at a primitive farmhouse, the only habitation around. Most of the action takes place inside the cabin's main room. All of these elements—the dark room, the crude house, the rural isolation, the fact that we are in the South—add to the story's meaning and impact.

As a story moves from scene to scene, the setting changes but always remains within the parameters of the story world. It's been said that short stories have a narrower range and reach than novels; with their limited length there's not enough room for running all over the earth. But a short story can be global in scope. As Shaila, protagonist of Bharati Mukherjee's *The Management of Grief*, copes with the deaths of her husband and sons, she moves from Toronto, to which the family had emigrated; to Ireland, off whose coast the fatal plane crash occurred; to her homeland of India; and back to Toronto again—all in the course of sixteen pages. What unites these disparate localities is the role they play in Shaila's search for personal definition. The story world consists of the stations on her journey from her old sense of self to her new one.

Occasionally the setting *is* the story. Ray Bradbury's short story, *There Will Come Soft Rains*, has all the elements of a dramatic narrative—except characters. This tale, amusing yet devastating in its effect, puts us inside a typical family home of the future on the day after the Bomb is dropped. No one is left. The automated devices that controlled the daily routines of the house and the family sputter on. The house and its contents become the characters; the story and the setting are one and the same.

Bradbury's story is extreme in eliminating human characters altogethe, but for many authors, the setting functions almost like another character. It is an active power that participates in shaping events, establishing a mood, and bringing readers into the story world.

Choosing Your Setting

"A story is in its setting because it could be nowhere else," award-winning mystery author Susan Dunlap often tells aspiring writers.

Sometimes the "nowhere else" is clear from the outset. An intriguing place triggers your imagination, providing the flour idea. Hiking up a rocky trail into a box canyon or driving past a Victorian mansion that is falling to ruin, you realize there must be a story here. Characters might stroll into your mind with their locales firmly attached. You know from the outset that she does social work in a Miami ghetto, that he herds cattle on a Montana ranch, that she attends school in an upscale suburban neighborhood, that he is a manager who pushes paper in a corporate high-rise, that she is a cop who walks a gritty city beat.

At other times you may need to think hard to figure out just where your story's "nowhere else" could be. You have a premise and a character or two, but they won't come alive because you haven't found the right place to put them. How do you know where they belong?

NEW SETTING EQUALS NEW STORY

A good story is a successful blend of people, plot, and place. Ask yourself: Where could this kind of situation arise? Where would someone like this be living or working or hanging out?

If you aren't sure, try the "what if..." game. A good use of "what if..." is to test your people and your premise in various settings. Let's try an experiment. Choose a character and a situation from a story of your own or one you've recently read. Now write a series of short paragraphs, installing the character in each of the locations below. Write in the first person from the character's point of view, having him or her describe the place and how it affects the story situation. Would it be the same story?

In the setting where the story takes place.

In a Beverly Hills neighborhood where the rich and famous dwell in lavish homes.

In a very poor, rundown neighborhood in Manhattan's Lower East Side.

In an isolated farming community where strangers are seldom seen.

On a small open boat traveling down the Amazon River.

In the marketplace in ancient Rome.

As you move the character from place to place, does the premise still work? Will you have the same story?

Probably not. When you change the setting, the story changes too, in ways that could be either subtle or grand. Put the same person and the same situation in ten different settings, and ten different stories will result.

THE INTERACTION OF PEOPLE AND PLACE

Places shape people, and people shape places. This is why the effect of your choice of setting is so profound. The interaction of characters and setting plays a big role in determining what the story is.

Take Jerry, a fifty-year-old flower child who has never recovered from the Summer of Love. He still dresses in tie-dye shirts and pulls back his hair, what's left of it, into a ponytail. Years ago he played bass in a rock band called the Bamboozles, dreaming of hitting the big time. The band came within a hair's breadth of signing with a big-name record company, but the deal collapsed at the last minute. Disheartened, the Bamboozles split up. Jerry drifted around for a while and ended up in Los Angeles, where for years he has grubbed out a living as a hardware store clerk. Now and then he sits in with a combo that jams in a local bar and sighs over what might have been. Now his mother, who lives a long distance away, is dying. Jerry moves into her house because she has no one else to take care of her. His goal is to care for his mother while creating a satisfying new life for himself.

Suppose Jerry's mother lives in San Francisco. From the moment he arrives in the city, he fits right in. When he walks to the market near his mother's home, no one pays much attention to his long hair, his psychedelic shirt, or the peace sign hanging from a leather cord around his neck. Most likely he'll find a network of kindred spirits without much trouble, including plenty of out-of-work musicians who will commiserate with him and perhaps invite him to join them on an occasional gig. His new friends and activities might well interfere with his giving proper care and attention to his mother.

What if we move Jerry to a Pennsylvania coal-mining town? He grew up there but, feeling stifled and longing for adventure, he dropped out of high school and fled. When he lugs his duffel bag into his childhood home and greets his dying mother, it's the first time he's been back in three decades. In this town Jerry stands apart. His demeanor, his mode of dress, his habits and tastes mark him as odd. Even though his mother's neighbors agree he is a dutiful son, they may view him with suspicion, skepticism, or disdain. He will have a harder time creating that satisfying new life here.

Same character, same situation, same goal. All we've changed is the setting. Either place could give you a compelling story, but it will play out very differently in San Francisco than in Coalmont, Pennsylvania. The location will influence the complications Jerry encounters and the choices he makes.

Examining the interaction of person and place can help you develop your story. Here are three perspectives to consider:

■ **The character's reaction to the place.** Has this person lived a long time in the area, or is he a visitor, a newcomer? Natives and strangers notice and respond to different things. Longtime residents have greater knowledge about a place, but they take for granted sights, sounds, and quirks of culture that an outsider finds novel or colorful or strange.

Here's an example: When I moved from the East Coast to Oklahoma, my new neighbors asked what impressed me most about their state. I replied, "The sky." They thought I was crazy; surely I'd had a sky overhead back east. Yes, but Oklahoma's was a different kind of sky, a vast sweep of blue with sunsets that spread around a full 360 degrees. The sky I was accustomed to was smaller and hazier, hemmed in by buildings and tall trees.

To depict a setting more vividly, consider making at least one character a stranger there. This person's observations can draw the reader's attention to details that a local wouldn't even notice. This works with the smallest-scale settings as well as with large ones. Suppose your story concerns a pair of elderly people, one of them a chain smoker, who have shared a tiny apartment for many years and rarely go out anymore. Smoke hangs in the air like a mist; its smell clings to the heavy drapes and overstuffed upholstery. Neither of the inhabitants is aware of it, not even the non-smoker, because it has been part of their environment for so long. When a long-lost grandson arrives, he, and through him the reader, will immediately be struck by the thick air and strong odor.

The character's emotional response to the place is equally as important as his sense of familiarity or strangeness. Does he feel comfortable here or out of his element? Is he an insider or an outsider? A person's attitude toward a place has little to do with the amount of time he's spent there. We can fall in love with a locale at first sight, or dislike a place where we've lived for years.

- **The reaction of the place to the character.** In most places, people are part of the environment, and your protagonist must deal with their reactions to him—their level of knowledge about him, their attitude toward him, and their degree of affinity to the kind of person he is.

This is one reason Jerry's story would change drastically if you moved it from San Francisco to Coalmont. The residents in these two locales are likely to differ in their backgrounds, lifestyles, and concepts of proper behavior. As a result they will have diverging opinions about Jerry and the sacrifice, if that's what it is, that he's making on his mother's behalf. Jerry's goal, remember, is twofold: to take care of his mother and to create a satisfying new life for himself. Whether he's in the big city or the small town, the reactions of the people around him will set up complications for him; the nature of the complications will depend on which part of his goal they choose to support or oppose.

The reaction of the place to your protagonist is a good source to check when you're looking for the conflict your protagonist faces. In what ways is she at odds with the environment? The answer to this question can inspire the creation of your antagonist or a strong secondary character who personifies the local point of view.

■ **Environmental circumstances to which the character must respond.** To a large extent, the place where they are dictates people's behavior. Our choices for action are constrained by such factors as the weather, the terrain, the nearness of neighbors, the distances between important points, and the objects that we do or don't have at hand. Eudora Welty's traveling salesman might have enjoyed a different fate if his car accident had occurred someplace where there was a telephone.

Even such simple matters as the clothes we wear are determined by our setting. Once I hiked down a trail from the top of a waterfall to the pool below. It was not long, only a mile or so, but it was steep. The footing was treacherous, with lots of soft sand and loose pebbles, and I was glad to have sturdy boots. At the bottom I encountered a young woman in high heels and a flowered dress, looking as if she had just arrived from church. What was she doing there, I wondered, and how was she going to climb back up without breaking an ankle? In other words, what was her story?

Such incongruities—people and things that are out of place in their environment—are a rich vein of fiction material. The setting offers both writer and characters an abundance of resources and challenges.

ACTUAL SETTINGS: FICTIONALIZING A PLACE THAT'S REAL

Should you choose a real place or an imaginary one in which to set your story?

One could argue that there is no such thing as a real setting. An author who sets a story in an actual place uses it as a model on which to base a story world. He selects certain details, ignores others, and invents still more, bending reality to suit the needs of the story. The place depicted in fiction may bear considerable resemblance to the one on the map, but it is being viewed through a filter or a lens that distorts it, if ever so slightly.

At a writers' conference, I appeared on a panel with five other authors who have written about San Francisco to discuss how we used the city as a setting. One of the group liked to play upon the cliches—the tourist attractions, the reputation for quirky behavior. Another preferred to take readers to corners of town they'd likely never discover on their own—warehouse districts, industrial zones, and rundown neighborhoods. Each of us drew our characters from different population groups. Finally one colleague pointed out, "What's clear is that we don't write about the same city at all. Read our works and you'll visit six different San Franciscos." We all fabricated the fictional city that would best serve the theme, mood, and tone of our own stories. Yet someone familiar with the city would find that each of these San Franciscos rings true.

Using an existing place as your setting gives you several advantages. First, it gives you lots of raw material to work with—props and scenery and characters and story ideas. It also assists in reader identification. People enjoy reading about locales they know, which is why books tend to sell well in the cities or regions where they are set. There is a pleasure in reading about a beach and knowing you've felt that very same sand between your bare toes, or encountering a description of a sidewalk cafe almost exactly like the one you frequented during your student days in Paris.

In exchange for these advantages, using a real setting obligates you to be accurate. Because readers are familiar with real places, they will recognize when you get them right. If you get something wrong, they will also notice and they'll call you on it. Worse, they might then distrust the rest of what you say.

The appropriate balance between authenticity and fictional license depends on your particular story. You must get the flavor and feel of the place right. What often works is to go ahead and invent the micro-environment while keeping the macro-environment intact. In other words, take liberties with the smaller elements—replace the building on the corner with one of your own, open a business, install a new street or a park, as long as you make them consistent with the kinds of buildings, businesses, and infrastructure that would be found in the real place. At the same time, keep the large identifying characteristics in place. These include not only the geography, the landmarks, and the neighborhoods, but cultural elements and ambiance as well.

When you choose an imaginary setting, you have the fun of creating a wholly imagined place, whether it's a town, a nation, a planet, or a magic realm. Part of the appeal of writing science fiction and fantasy is in challenging your creative powers to invent new technologies, new cultures, new species, and entire new worlds. For some stories, there is no actual, existing place where they could happen.

With an imaginary setting, you don't have to worry so much about accuracy. After all, if you've made the whole place up, no one can accuse you of getting it wrong. All we know about it is what you tell us. What's more, you and your characters are not hemmed in by a real place's unfortunate or inconvenient features. You can bend geography to your will, manipulating it to satisfy the demands of your plot.

Of course these benefits have a downside: You must explain everything. You get no help from the readers' previous knowledge or understanding, the way you would if you used a real location. It is a large task to successfully transplant something that exists solely in your own mind into the minds of your readers, so that we can see it, hear it, smell it, and wander around in it as easily as you do. Even though your marvelous place doesn't exist, you must convince us it does; you must realize it fully enough that we believe in it.

This means you must know it well enough to describe it not only comprehensively but consistently. Internal consistency is essential to making an invented place credible. Once you have established a "fact" about your imaginary place, that fact should hold true throughout the story. The place also must operate according to some sort of logic. This does not necessarily have to be real-world logic; a fantasy realm could adhere to a logic system all its own. But once you have established the system's rules, you must follow them.

Bringing Your Setting to Life

One of the rewards of reading fiction is being able, by melding our imagination with the author's, to unshackle ourselves from the here and now and experience a new and intriguing parallel universe. Readers are willing participants in this process, the more so when the author makes the world we enter vivid and accessible. Whether your setting is large-scale or small-scale, imaginary or real, these techniques will help you bring it to life.

I. MAKE THE PLACE THREE-DIMENSIONAL.

Just as three-dimensional characters come alive for readers, so do three-dimensional settings. When you incorporate aspects of all three dimensions into your depiction of setting, your story world becomes more realistic and vibrant.

- **Physical.** The physical environment encompasses all the factors our senses can discern—sizes and shapes, colors and textures, scents and sounds. For large-scale settings, it includes climate, terrain, natural features, and all the ways human beings have put their stamp upon the land. On a smaller scale, physical characteristics might include the furnishings within a room, the size of the windows, and the angle at which sunlight comes in.
- **Sociological.** The sociological environment comprises the cultural, economic, and political characteristics of the place and its typical inhabitants. It reflects the residents' understanding and experience of the world they live in, and their beliefs and attitudes about people and societal roles.
- **Psychological.** Places have personalities. The house on the corner is dreary; the bungalow next door is cheerful. This neighborhood is a wild and crazy place, but the one across town is stodgy and dull. The psychological environment provides much of a setting's atmosphere.

These three environmental dimensions blend to give a place its distinctive nature. A town on a riverbank has industries and recreational facilities that take advantage of this resource. The nationality of the early settlers is imprinted on local food delicacies, festivals, and the architectural style of the historic buildings along Main Street. The university that dominates the town has attracted residents with certain interests, attitudes, biases, and worldviews, and these are different than they would be if the town's major institution were a prison.

108

The Tip Sheet: Three Dimensional Settings on page 115 lists some of the components that contribute to the physical, sociological, and psychological dimensions of setting. It asks some questions that can help you determine what a place is like and how you might use its attributes in your story.

The tip sheet applies most obviously to regions, cities, or neighborhoods, but the factors listed are just as pertinent if you are working on a smaller scale. Suppose you have chosen a narrow setting: the office building where your protagonist, Elliott, works. The town where it's located is anonymous and nondescript because larger layers of setting are irrelevant to your plot.

The building itself provides the physical environment—its style, its surroundings, its features, its comfort level. Is it a sleek new high-rise or an older building that has suffered years of neglect? Is it cheek-to-jowl with other buildings on a bustling city street or does it sit in lonely splendor amidst acres of parked cars? Do the elevators and air conditioning operate smoothly or conk out regularly? Does Elliott enjoy a corner office with a rosewood desk and an oriental carpet, or does he toil in a cubicle with a gray laminate slab for a work surface and a chair that strains his back?

The nature of the company creates the sociological environment. What is the product or service? This determines the kinds of work performed and the types of people who are Elliott's coworkers. Other contributing factors include the financial fortunes of the firm and its reputation within its industry. Then there's the power structure and Elliott's position within it—not only the organizational chart but the informal systems by which things really get done.

The psychological environment is a product of the corporate culture. Companies have different values and philosophies and standards of conduct; they vary in their management styles and levels of morale. Elliott's firm might take a casual and free-wheeling approach to work, rewarding innovation and encouraging friendships among the employees; or it might foment rivalries and insist that established procedures be followed strictly. All of these factors combine to yield distinctive business personalities.

Or consider a house. It has obvious physical characteristics: age, size, style, the materials from which it was built, the items that furnish and decorate it. It even has its own climate: hot or cold, dry or damp. But a house is a sociological and psychological environment as well. It bears the imprint of its occupants— their relationships, styles, interests, and attitudes. Even in a suburban tract of cookie-cutter homes with identical floor plans, the houses take on individuality. The way they are furnished and used reflects the lives lived within them.

2. TREAT TIME AS THE FOURTH DIMENSION.

Time adds a fourth dimension to your setting, as important as the three dimensions that characterize the place. Day or night, summer or winter, today or two hundred years ago—you can use time to establish an atmosphere, provide complications, and influence the characters' choices and actions.

As time passes, the characteristics of a place change. When you write a story set in the past or the future, your concern is not the physical, sociological, and psychological aspects of the setting as they are now, but as they were then or as they will become.

Until we are all issued crystal balls, your predictions for the future are as valid as anyone's. If your story takes place many years from now, let your inventiveness fly; what you have is an imaginary setting and the same considerations apply. You have somewhat less license if you are projecting a real place forward just a decade or two. You'll want to extrapolate what's to come from what already exists. To determine what can reasonably be anticipated, couple your knowledge of the place as it is today with your awareness of cultural, political, economic, and technological trends. Of course readers can do this, too. If you deviate too far from conclusions they've drawn, you'll have to persuade them that a logical sequence of events has taken your chosen locale from the known *now* to your fantasy of *then*.

With a historical setting you have all the demands for accuracy that a real setting entails, plus the added challenge of getting the period details right. Whatever decade or century you choose, there are bound to be readers who are familiar with it and who will catch your anachronisms and other errors. To make your story true to its time, you will need to know the period as well as you know the place. The physical, sociological, and psychological environments of a given locale can alter immeasurably over the years, and the amount of time required for major change to take place can be surprisingly short.

The more remote in time and place your setting is, the harder it becomes to research the details that support a three-dimensional presentation of the setting. Major events, such as battles and coronations, are well documented, and you may find information on the lives of the noble, rich, and famous. What's not easy to learn is how ordinary folks in distant times conducted their daily lives—how they did their laundry and what they ate for breakfast.

Perhaps the most difficult aspect of a time period to understand and convey is the collective social behavior, knowledge, and attitudes—the mind-set—of the people you're writing about. A common error is to impose today's beliefs and opinions (for example, that all humans are created equal, or that romantic love is a proper basis for marriage) on characters who live in a time or place where science or philosophy or religion do not yet permit such notions to be entertained. Not only would people of the past not have agreed with many modern ideas, they could not even have conceived of them. In much the same way, we find it difficult to comprehend what it would be like to base our lives on the absolute, perfect knowledge that the earth is flat and that a chariot of fire called the sun races around it.

"Getting the mind-set right is the hardest part of writing historical fiction," says Chelsea Quinn Yarbro, whose has written stories set on six continents and in most centuries from Etruscan times to the present. "The tricky part is not knowing what people did, but what they thought they were doing."

3. GIVE READERS THE EXPERIENCE OF BEING THERE.

It's time to invite readers to join you in your story world. These techniques will help you draw them in and keep them there:

■ **Orient your readers quickly.** As you open the story and at the beginning of each subsequent scene, give us a sense of the time and the place, not necessarily in every particular, but enough to give the action a context and let us visualize what's happening. If we can't create a mental picture, or the one we come up with is muddled and confused, we're likely to lose interest. This is how I opened my story, *Playing for Keeps*:

Oh good—voices from the upstairs playroom.

Nicola kicked the front door shut behind her. Rain began drumming on the porch roof; she had just missed getting soaked. She set her lunchbox on the entryway table and shrugged out of the jacket that had been Caroline's and the scarf that had been Graham's. Then she bounded up the stairs, two at a time, to find Jeffrey.

It was the best moment of the day, seeing Jeffrey.

"Nic, is that you?" Mother's voice. "Did you hang up your coat?"

"Yes, ma'am." Nicola trudged back downstairs and plucked the dumb old jacket off the floor.

Mother came into the living room, turning on the lamp by the sofa. It did little to dispel the November gloom. "How was school today?"

Right away readers know that we're in a multistoried family home, probably a large one since there are several children and room to spare for a playroom. It's November, late afternoon. We hear the rain, see the little girl's scattered belongings, notice the yellow glow against the darkness when the lamp comes on. We're standing there watching as Nicola and her mother interact.

■ **Pile on the details.** More than anything else, this is what creates the you-are-there experience for readers. Details are the hooks that connect our imaginations to your own. The more specific the better. The aggregation of small particulars creates the atmosphere and makes the setting vivid. When you mention that a windowbox is full of flowers, you're giving us information. Tell us that it's brimming with red geraniums and suddenly we're seeing the same thing that you and your characters see.

■ **Use all five senses.** Our senses are how we connect with the world and take in information about it, and this is true whether the world in question is real or fictional. The descriptive details that will be most effective are those that create strong sensory impressions, and not just visual ones. Although visual impressions are important, remember that we have five senses altogether. Bring in colors, light and dark, sounds, aromas, flavors, and textures. As the characters see, hear, smell, taste, and feel the various elements within their surroundings, readers will do so too. The more you trigger sensations from all five senses, the deeper and richer the readers' experience will become. See if you can find all five senses represented in this example:

A heavy scent of garlic and basil hit my nose as I followed Moira into the kitchen. She lifted the lid of a kettle on the stove, releasing a hot burst of steam. As it cleared she dipped in a ladle, which she handed to me. Thick red tomato sauce. For Tom's favorite lasagna, I was sure.

"Does it have enough salt?" she asked.

I lifted the spoon to my lips and tasted. Too much salt, in fact, and an overdose of garlic as well. "It's perfect," I said.

Moira retrieved a cutting board from a cabinet and set it down with a bang on the glazed tiles of the counter. "I'm avoiding the issue, aren't I? You came to tell me about Tom."

"Yes. But I...I don't know where to begin."

I clasped her hand but barely had time to register how cold it felt before she pulled it away. Refusing to look at me, she grabbed a sharp knife and began sawing on a loaf of crusty bread. "It's bad news, isn't it?"

■ **Choose details to suit your mood.** In a short story every word must pull its weight, so you want your details to do double duty. Not only should they make the surroundings seem real but, if possible, they should accomplish a second job—characterize someone, provide important information, or contribute to creating a certain atmosphere.

Imagine that you've placed a comic tale, a romance, a suspense story, and a tragic slice of life all in the same setting. For each story you'd choose different details to establish and reinforce the appropriate mood.

In Moira's kitchen the burst of steam, the bang of the cutting board against the tile, and the sharp knife are all intended to buttress the tension she feels and to help readers share it. If she were expecting a positive message about Tom, the details might be different. The tomato sauce would not be oversalted. The radio could be on, with romantic music playing. Rather than hard glazed tiles, readers' attention might be drawn to lace curtains or the silk shirt under Moira's apron.

■ **Show how your characters respond to this place and to the events happening there.** What makes a setting most vivid to readers is watching the characters in action within it and sharing their responses to it. Show what is happening to them physically and emotionally as well:

> Elizabeth wanted to cry as she watched Heather and Carina stride around the bend in the trail and disappear into the pines. She was the last one again, the perpetual straggler. She probably wouldn't make it back to Camp Miwok until all the other kids were already splashing in the pool. By the time she limped in, dirty and sweaty and red with sunburn, swimming hour would be over and she wouldn't even get to cool off before supper.
>
> There was no one around to watch, so she lifted the front of her T-shirt and used it to mop her dripping forehead. How could the stupid counselors have sent them off hiking on a day like this? One hundred and ten in the shade, it had to be. Elizabeth was wearing her shorts, but that didn't help. A few minutes ago, when she'd collapsed onto a rock to rest, the sun-baked surface had scorched her bare thighs as if she'd sat on a hot stove.
>
> Okay, head for the pines. At least there it would be shady. And camp couldn't be more than half a mile farther. One step, two steps, three steps. Drat. A stone in her boot, small but sharp, was digging into her left heel.

Feelings beget feelings. As the characters' experiences trigger memories of how we felt in similar circumstances, we empathize and identify with them more strongly.

This is a significant accomplishment. Establishing that intimacy with characters is one of the major reasons readers read and writers write.

Tip Sheet:
Three-Dimensional Settings

I. PHYSICAL ENVIRONMENT

Geography and terrain—Is the place mountainous, hilly, or flat? Is it rural, urban, or suburban? If it's the boonies, is it wilderness or farmland? What is its relation to water—is it next to an ocean, a lake, a river? Or landlocked and dry? What does a typical landscape look like?

Weather and climate—Hot, cold, dry, wet, windy, or calm? Does the place experience storms? If so, what kind? What is the most extreme weather? What is the seasonal variation? How does the weather differ from the norm (e.g., warm in the winter, cold and foggy in the summer)?

Flora and fauna—What kinds of plants and animals are typical of this place? How do they affect the place (e.g., gorgeous autumn leaves attract tourists; mountain lions at urban–rural interface points create a fear of danger)?

Built environment—How have humans made their impact? What are the architectural styles, housing types, other kinds of buildings? Streets, highways, roads—what are the traffic patterns? Where are the traffic jams?

2. SOCIOLOGICAL ENVIRONMENT

Types of people—What kinds of people live here? How do they interact? Are people very similar or do they represent many different backgrounds? Do people from different groups mingle or keep to their own kind?

Social and political climate—Who runs things? What is the power structure? Are people generally liberal or conservative? What are the key local issues? What are the hot buttons—the topics everybody reacts to emotionally?

Economic base and major industries—How do people around here earn their livings? What is the socioeconomic structure—a blue-collar town, rich estates for the upper-crust polo set?

Education—What level of education do people typically obtain? Do the locals value education or are they disdainful and suspicious of it? Are the local schools good or poor? What kinds of educational institutions are available?

Religion—What religions are represented here? Are there many or does one predominate? How important a role does religion play in people's lives?

Local taste—How do people dress? What, for instance, is typical business dress? (It's different in Los Angeles than in Washington, D.C.). What kinds of cars do people typically drive? What are the specialties of the local cuisine?

Holidays and celebrations—What special occasions does the community celebrate, and how? Are there annual parades or festivals? What kinds of events bring people together?

Arts, culture, and entertainment—What kinds of music, art, movies, TV, etc., are popular? What kinds of sports? How do people like to have fun? What sorts of facilities—theaters, museums, music organizations, playing fields, sports arenas—are available to people?

Crime patterns—What kind of crimes predominate? What is the crime rate? Is this place dangerous or safe? What is the general attitude toward law enforcement?

Image in the rest of the world—What image does the place have in the eyes of outsiders? What is it famous for? Do outsiders come in droves or stay away? What would its tourist board tout as a lure for visitors?

3. PSYCHOLOGICAL ENVIRONMENT

Prevailing viewpoints—How do the people in this place think? What kind of attitudes do they have? Are they trendsetters or laggards? What are the conventional wisdoms (the things everyone "knows" to be true, whether they really are or not)?

Normal behavior—What is considered to be normal behavior? How wide a range of behaviors is normal? What is considered to be deviant behavior?

Attitude toward differences—How do people respond to deviations from normal behavior? Are they tolerant or intolerant? Are they welcoming of strangers? What happens to someone who is "different"?

Local legends, local heroes—Whom do the people here admire, and why?

Emotional impact—What kind of emotional response does being in this place evoke in its inhabitants? In visitors?

Personality—What key words would sum up the personality of this place?

Exercises: Making a Setting Vivid

1. Choose three short stories to read and think about. For each story, write brief answers to the following questions:

    a. How important is the setting to this story?

    b. To what extent does the author bring in physical, sociological, and psychological dimensions of the place where the story occurs?

    c. How does the setting influence the events of the story, or of particular scenes?

    d. Would you consider the setting to be a character in this story? Why or why not?

    e. If you changed the setting, how would the story change?

    f. What kinds of details does the author provide about places in the story? Do the chosen details fit the story and the characters? How might the choice of details change if this were a different kind of story?

    g. What sensory impressions does the author evoke? Find examples of the use of all five senses.

    h. How well did the author succeed in bringing you into the story world?

2. Choose a location that is familiar to you, for instance, a room in your home, workplace, or school. Write five paragraphs, describing this place in each of the following ways:

    Paragraph 1: A straight, objective description.

    Paragraph 2: As if you were writing a comic story or a spoof.

    Paragraph 3: As if you were writing a romance.

    Paragraph 4: As if you were writing a mystery or suspense story.

    Paragraph 5: As if you were writing a horror story.

3. Read *The Life of the Party* on page 53 and decide what kind of party this is and where it is taking place. Rewrite the scene from the point of view of one of the characters, emphasizing

the setting. Feel free to add details; you don't need to stick to the events described. For example, the party could be:

- A political fund-raiser at a California winery or in a New York City hotel.
- A barbecue on a Texas ranch or in a suburban backyard in the Northeast.
- A New Year's Eve party in San Francisco, Boston, Honolulu, or Houston.

4. Pick a sensory impression—a color, a texture, a sound, a scent, or a taste. Imagine a location where you might experience that impression. Using the sensory impression as a jumping-off point, write a brief scene that takes place there.

5. Write three separate paragraphs describing the town where you grew up. In each paragraph, emphasize a different dimension:

   Paragraph 1: The physical environment.

   Paragraph 2: The sociological environment.

   Paragraph 3: The psychological environment.

6. Set a timer for five minutes. Copy the following passage and, when you reach the ellipsis(...), keep writing without lifting your pen from the paper or your fingers from the keyboard. Continue the story, telling what happens next, until the timer sounds. Try to bring in impressions from all five senses.

   When I got home, I went into my room. At first I didn't notice anything wrong. Then my heart jumped into my throat, because suddenly...

7. Select a scene from a story you have written or one you wrote for an exercise in this book. Rewrite the scene in a totally new setting. Keep the characters and the situation the same as much as possible, but change them as the new setting demands.

Chapter 6

Narrative Voice

How to Develop Your Individual Voice As a Writer

Several years ago, when I was editing the newsletter of a local writers' organization, a business trip took me to New York. Seizing the opportunity, I extended my visit by several days and set up interviews with a dozen fiction editors at major publishing houses. Later I wrote up our discussions in a market report for my fellow members.

One question I asked the editors was what they look for in a work of fiction, what qualities would land a manuscript in the "buy" pile. They concurred on four points:

- Characters who come to life,
- A vivid setting,
- An intriguing subject or background, and
- A strong, original voice.

"Voice?" I asked. "What do you mean by voice?"

They answered with lots of hemming and hawing. Not one of them could come up with a definition, but every one cited it as a major element in the stories that grabbed them. They agreed that voice, whatever it is, makes a story distinctive and unique. A powerful voice lifts the story above the crowd of pages that editors read and makes it linger in memory. One reason editors seek it out is because it can lead to good reviews and stronger sales for the work in question.

Since then I've thought a lot about the elusive quality called voice. If it is so important to a successful story, I want to make it sing in my own stories and also help other writers understand it.

What Is Voice?

Voice, I've concluded, is different from the other four main ingredients of fiction. Character, conflict, plot, and setting, taken together, are the story. Voice is how you tell it.

Voice is the manner in which you combine ideas and language to create a dramatic effect or elicit the desired response from the reader.

Voice is the sum of all the decisions you make, consciously and unconsciously, about words and paragraphs and rhythm and tone and style.

Voice is the way you imbue the story with your singular perspectives, insights, and attitudes.

Voice is what makes your writing sound like you.

THE QUALITIES OF VOICE

Every writer has an individual voice, a natural and personal mode of expressing ideas. When you first take on the challenge of writing fiction, you may sound tentative, unsure, and ordinary. As you keep writing and your skills and confidence grow, your narrative voice will develop too, becoming stronger, fresher, and more original.

Authors' voices vary in much the same way characters' voices do. One writer may be terse while another is garrulous. This one is straightforward and direct, but that one hints obliquely at actions and their meanings. Writers choose different styles, ranging from casual to formal, from lean to lush, from dark to light.

In Chapter One, we called narrative voice the "artful way" a story is told. I've identified seventeen qualities that contribute to that artfulness—the constituents of narrative voice. The list is not necessarily exhaustive; you may be able to think of more. Nor is it prescriptive; it is not meant to imply that you must handle any of these things in a particular way. The list simply pinpoints some of the choices a writer makes in deciding how best to present the story:

1. Choice of words.
2. Structure and arrangement of sentences and paragraphs.
3. Rhythm of the language.
4. Degree of formality in the language.
5. Linear versus layered narrative structure.
6. Balance among action, dialogue, description, and exposition.
7. Use of details.
8. Level of suspense.
9. Pace of the story.
10. Amount and kind of humor.
11. Amount of emotional color.
12. Regional or cultural flavor.
13. Use of imagery, metaphor, and simile.
14. Use of symbols.
15. Kinds of allusions and references in the story.
16. The worldview implicit in the story.
17. The consistency with which the voice is maintained.

The Tip Sheet: Narrative Voice on page 134 provides a more complete understanding of these qualities. Questions are listed that define each category. When you read a short story, these questions can help you analyze how the author tries to achieve an impact—and whether to your mind he succeeds. When you are writing a short story, they can suggest the many possible tools you can use to express your vision clearly and powerfully.

THE VOICE OF THE STORY

A good story demands its own voice.

No two stories you write will sound alike. Each has its own characters, setting, atmosphere, and series of events. Therefore it requires its own system of telling, a voice that will capitalize on the unmatched opportunities offered by these ingredients placed in this configuration. Of course you would modify your voice to suit the genre of story you're writing, whether it's mainstream, mystery, science fiction, or romance, whether it's a humorous tale or a serious one. Even stories that are similar on the surface, though, may inspire different choices about certain qualities of narrative voice.

The most significant factor in choosing a voice is your protagonist. In telling the story you adjust the voice of the story in one of three ways:

■ **To accentuate the main character's voice.** In a first person story or a third person story told from the protagonist's point of view, her voice is the story voice. You present the story in her language and style. Doing this reinforces the intimacy between the character and the readers.

■ **To contrast with the main character's voice.** Sometimes the most effective way to characterize the protagonist, or to offer your desired perspective on her and the events in which she plays a role, is to use a voice that is pointedly dissimilar from hers. You can do this from a third person omniscient point of view, but it is also a good reason for assigning the job of narrator to some character other than the protagonist.

■ **To make your presentation seem objective.** Describing the events in a neutral voice allows readers to draw their own conclusions about the protagonist and the story—seemingly without your guidance, even though you are there behind the scenes throughout the story, directing our response. In *Hunters in the Snow*, Tobias Wolff describes three buddies who are out for a day of winter hunting when something goes terribly wrong. We never really hear the hunters' thoughts or get inside their heads. Instead we are shown what transpires and allowed to form our own opinions. The story voice is consistently impartial and nonjudgmental; the reader's reaction, though, is strong.

Making Your Voice Stronger

Your best assets as a writer are a lively curiosity and a love of language. They are the wellsprings of a powerful narrative voice.

Curiosity fuels the imagination. While someone else might see what you do and ignore it, curiosity nudges you in the ribs and asks, "What if...?" It pushes you to take a closer, harder look not only at what strikes you as strange but at what seems familiar or commonplace. When you cultivate your curiosity—by learning new things, going to new places, meeting new people, listening to new points of view—it rewards you with ideas and insights from which you can create compelling stories.

Language, with all its sprawling, hurly-burly exuberance, its rules and exceptions to rules, its bounds and the leaps that take it beyond the bounds, its color and flash and stillness and motion, is the stuff that your writer's voice is made of. Language gives you the means to express your ideas and insights, to throw open the doors of your imagination and let people enter. Your job as a writer is to use language with precision and purpose. As you learn to control it and make it do your bidding, your voice will become stronger and surer.

Here are some suggestions to help you develop a clear, vigorous, and confident narrative voice:

I. KNOW THE FUNDAMENTALS OF HOW LANGUAGE WORKS.

If you're not certain about grammar, brush up. Far from being a boring, arcane list of do's and don'ts, grammar is a dynamic system of extraordinary beauty and power. It is the design that transforms a series of words from a meaningless list into the expression of a thought. Grammar is what makes verbal communication possible.

Understanding the rules of grammar and usage doesn't require you to adhere slavishly to them. But readers can tell the difference between an author who breaks the rules deliberately to achieve a purpose, and one who doesn't know or care what he's doing.

For guidance, try *The Elements of Style* by William Strunk, Jr. and E.B. White. This slender volume, which has become a classic in the decades since it was first published, is a succinct and authoritative guide to presenting ideas with clarity and flair. You might also want to add to your reference shelf two books by Karen Elizabeth Gordon: *The Deluxe Transitive Vampire* and *The New Well-Tempered Sentence*. These peculiarly named works offer sound advice on grammar and punctuation respectively, yet demonstrate the rules with flights of fantasy so that these seemingly dry subjects become whimsical and fun.

2. FALL IN LOVE WITH WORDS.

Words are your basic tools. Your stories benefit when you appreciate how words work, keep them sharp and polished, and use them with care and accuracy.

Writers delight in words the way skilled cabinetmakers take pleasure in beautifully crafted implements for their trade. Writers enjoy word games. They read dictionaries for fun. Okay, they may not curl up with one in front of the fire, but when double-checking a word they get caught up by intriguing new words and their meanings, derivations, and relationships to other words.

One could say that writing is a simple matter of putting the right words in the right order. The trick, of course, is figuring out at every point exactly what the right words are. Here are a few pointers that might help you decide:

■ **Use active words.** Count on verbs to do your heavy lifting. Verbs contain action, and therefore energy. This gives them greater strength and power than the other parts of speech. Changing the verb in a sentence alters the impact of what you're saying. Notice the difference in the picture created in following examples:

"Don't open the door," said Lee. Too late—Terry had turned the knob .The door swung open and...

"Don't open the door," yelled Lee. Too late—Terry had yanked the knob. The door slammed open and...

"D-don't open the door," stammered Lee. Too late—Terry had twisted the knob. The door creaked open and...

We don't know what's behind the door, but our expectations about what it could be shift a bit with each variation. Limit your use of *is* and *was*, *have* and *had*. Although they are verbs, the variants of *to be* and *to have* are passive—they just sit there. Try to visualize the phrase *there is...*, and you

126

draw a blank. If you can, find a way to express the thought so that readers can see it vividly:

Gina was a happy woman who had long black hair.

Gina always tossed back her long black hair when she laughed, something she did often.

- **Be careful with adjectives and adverbs.** They can be valuable assistants, but too often writers rely on them to do a job that could be handled better by an aptly chosen noun or verb.

  Nathan *went slowly* down the sidewalk.
  Nathan...meandered, drifted, sauntered, strolled, ambled, hobbled, plodded...down the sidewalk.

  Todd *went quickly* down the sidewalk.
  Todd...jogged, ran, dashed, rushed, sprinted, galloped, raced...down the sidewalk.

Each of the verbs conveys a slightly different image of Nathan or Todd, and a more specific picture than the combination of *went* with its adverb.

After you write a scene, try cutting out all adjectives and adverbs and then read both versions out loud. Put back only the modifiers that provide essential information or contribute to the vividness of the readers' mental picture.

- **Be wary of waffle words.** Language with impact is straightforward. Qualifiers like *somewhat, rather,* and *very* can detract more than they add, making prose sound wishy-washy and indecisive. They undercut the impact of the words they modify.

Don't hedge your bets with *maybe, might have,* or *seems.* Avoid phrases like, "It seems as if there might be a unicorn in the garden." If you see a mythical beast prancing amongst the tulips, say so with conviction.

The exception is in dialogue. When you put words like this in someone's mouth, it can characterize her as hesitant, unassertive, or insecure.

■ **Accept responsibility and give credit where it's due.** Business writing coaches rail at a fault that creeps all too often into on-the-job memos, letters, and reports: the use of passive voice instead of active voice. While this is troublesome in professional writing, it's death in fiction. What are active and passive voice? In the active voice, somebody performs an action. In the passive voice, the action just sort of happens.

This is a problem in stories for two reasons. One is that passive-voice writing is vague. It does not lend itself to sensory impressions. The actions it depicts are incomplete and blurry, and therefore hard to visualize. The other is that it breaks the chain of actions and consequences. In passive voice, you have an effect without a cause. No one is willing to take the responsibility for it, or the credit. For example:

> *Active voice:* The board of directors decided to adopt the proposed policy.

> *Passive voice:* It was decided that the proposed policy would be adopted.

Reading the passive-voice version in the minutes of the meeting, you can almost hear the board members saying, "What decision? What policy? Hey, it wasn't my fault."

People who write a lot in the course of their jobs are sometimes surprised to find that it's hard to make the transition to writing fiction. One reason is that caution is a driving force in business writing. This is why passive voice, which can sidestep issues and provide a mask of anonymity, is so popular—and so frustrating. Fiction writing, on the other hand, requires boldness, daring, a willingness to make strong statements and take risks.

■ **Watch out for your favorite pets, default options, and verbal tics.** We all have them—words and phrases we especially like, or that come so naturally we use them without thinking. They may be excellent choices, elegant, vibrant and strong. The problem is that because they flow so easily, we tend to overuse them, sometimes to the point of sounding repetitive, careless, and even dull.

Consider these to be your own personal cliches. Letting them pop up from time to time in a story may be fine, as long as they don't appear twice in a paragraph or three times on a page. Be careful, though, not to lean on them too heavily. Stretch yourself to find a new, fresh way to make the point.

■ **Look beyond the word's meaning.** It's been said that there is no such thing as a synonym. Words have color, tone, emotional weight and connotations beyond their literal definitions. They have strengths and weaknesses. They have sounds and rhythms that might be harmonious or discordant in a particular passage or story. Change the word and you will change the impression you make on your readers.

Consider, for example, the words and phrases in this list:

Naked, nude, bare, undressed, unclothed, stripped, in the buff, in the raw, in his birthday suit.

They all mean the same thing: The emperor is not wearing any clothes. Yet as we substitute one word for another, our perceptions of the character and the circumstances shift, and so do our feelings about them.

Here are some more examples. In the sentences below, think about the subtle ways in which switching the words alters the response generated:

As the hours dragged on and the jury still didn't return, Peterson grew ever more...worried, uneasy, nervous, fretful, edgy, jittery, antsy, jumpy.

Wishing her pillow were Blake, Susannah picked it up off the bed and...held it close, held it tight, hugged it, embraced it, caressed it, fondled it, squeezed it.

They knew the beast was somewhere out there in the darkness. As they huddled in the tiny tent, they could hear it...yell, shout, moan, howl, scream, bellow, holler, shriek, cry, roar.

Choosing the right word means paying attention to its effect as well as its meaning.

■ **Make every word count.** If your object is to put the right words in the right order, then it follows that each and every word must earn its keep. You can't afford freeloaders, weaklings, or lazy bums that tag along for the ride but don't contribute to the story.

You'll recall that in Chapter One we talked about writing three drafts. One thing that distinguishes the three drafts is how you handle words in each one.

The first draft is the what-to-say draft. At this stage you can be profligate; enjoy the luxury of using a wealth of words as you figure out your story. Give yourself permission to use words that are murky, imprecise, or just plain wrong. Lock your infernal internal editor in the desk drawer. Right now you're in exploration mode. Your mission is to discover the story's ideas and issues, become acquainted with your characters, and watch them in action to see what they'll do.

By the time you begin round two, the how-to-say-it draft, the story will be firmly in place in your mind, even if it's still shaky on paper. Now you can begin to look at your use of language. Team up with your internal editor to make sure you're choosing the words and images with the greatest punch and power, the ones that will convey your ideas most clearly and truthfully.

The third draft is cut-and-polish time, much as if you were transforming a rough stone into a glistening gem. Test each word: Is it accurate? Is it strong? Is it necessary?

One of my short stories came in at 2,300 words when I finished it. I liked it and so did others; it won a minor prize. Some time later I decided to submit it to a market that placed a 1,500-word cap on story length. I chopped out almost 800 words, a full one-third of the original story, convinced I was removing muscle and bone along with any fat. It wasn't published and I put it away. Recently, ready to send it out again, I reread both versions. I realized that the shorter one was far better—tighter, tenser, faster, sharper than the original.

It can be difficult and frustrating to change words and, worse, to slice them away when each was so hard-won. But the story is usually the better for it.

3. USE WORDS TO SHOW, NOT TELL.

Introducing me as a guest speaker in a sixth-grade class-room, the teacher asked the students if they could tell me the number one rule for creative writing. In one voice, twenty-seven excited kids yelled out: "Show, don't tell!"

Perhaps it's not the number one rule (There are no rules, remember?), but it's pretty good advice.

The difference between showing and telling is this:

Telling: Katie was humiliated when the other kids laughed at her. She tried to tell them that what happened wasn't her fault.

Showing: The other kids were all staring at her, and some of them had their hands over their mouths to hide their smirks and giggles. Katie felt the blood rush to her face and knew she was turning bright red ."It wasn't my fault," she tried to say, but the words made her choke. Salty tears stung her eyes. She blinked hard to keep them from sliding down her face, but it didn't work.

In writing a story, you have four ways to give the reader information: action, dialogue, description, and exposition. When you use action and dialogue, you are showing. When you provide description and exposition—background information and explanations of what's going on—you are telling.

When you show readers what's happening, you keep us firmly inside the story, participating in the events. You evoke in us the feelings of your protagonist or viewpoint character, or the memory of those feelings, increasing our sense of identification with her. In the example above, our empathy with Katie increases when we are shown, not just told, the predicament she's in.

Telling keeps us at arm's length. Pauses in the action, even to give us important information, can pull us back out of the story world. A friend of mine gripes when she reads a story and encounters what she calls expository lumps—points when the action stops while the author spoonfeeds us large chunks of information.

You avoid this problem when you take the gravy approach to fiction writing: Stir tidbits of description and exposition into the action and dialogue, blending them all smoothly and smashing up any big lumps.

Showing may require more words than telling, yet it's faster reading. A short story writer doesn't have the luxury of space that a novelist does, so at times you'll need to summarize crucial information for the readers' benefit. But as much as you can, use these gravy-making techniques:

- **Think in scenes.** Structure your story as a series of scenes that fix both characters and readers firmly in a particular time and place. Move quickly from one scene to the next, without lengthy transitions.

- **Keep the action going.** Weave in the background material a line or two at a time. That way you don't give readers a chance to wander away from the scene.

- **Let the characters do the explaining.** Put important information in dialogue and give us the pleasure of discovering it by eavesdropping. Let one character explain things to another who needs the information as much as we do.

- **Use flashbacks.** If we need to know about a salient background incident, time-travel us back to the moment when it occurred. Make the flashback a little scene of its own, with characters in action in a specific time and place.

4. RESPECT THE POWER OF LANGUAGE.

Language has magic powers. It can provoke us, engage our hearts and minds, or convince us to believe in something. It can delight or frighten us, and move us to laughter or tears. It can admit us into the realm of someone else's imagination and make us care about the fortunes of people who do not exist.

The power of language in fiction derives from the seventeen qualities of narrative voice. Experiment with them; stretch yourself by trying out new modes of expression. Apply your lively curiosity to language and its powers and possibilities. Your reward will be a writer's voice with which you can make magic.

Making Your Voice Your Own

Imitation may be the sincerest form of flattery, but mimicking another writer does not make for good writing any more than copying a portrait by an Old Master makes for great art. Analyzing how a certain writer uses language to achieve effects can be beneficial as you experiment with narrative voice. So can understanding the conventions and expectations of the genre you're writing in. But it is a mistake to assume that what works for someone else will necessarily work for you.

You might be thinking, *But all science fiction stories are like this,* or *This is how a mystery is supposed to sound,* or *If I don't do it this way, it won't be literary.* It's true that stories in a given genre have commonalities; the common threads define the category. If you want to write in that genre, read stories of that kind voluminously until you've absorbed their form and feel into your bones. Then write the same kind of story, but differently. Do it your way.

To find out what your way is, ignore the trends and pursue the story you feel passionate about. Make yourself a sorcerer's apprentice, learning how language makes magic. Become willing to offer your unique and valuable perspective, based on your personal observations, experiences, and imaginings, and to do it with no holds barred.

Your characters, conflict, plot, and setting embody your ideas and insights. What you are striving to do is communicate them to readers with the greatest possible impact and power. This is what editors are responding to when they cite voice as a key to a successful story.

There are three proven ways to develop your voice as a writer. When you follow these steps you will gain confidence and achieve better control over your material. Your appreciation of language will grow and so will your skill in using it.

1. Write.

2. Write some more.

3. Keep on writing.

Enjoy your journey into your story world.

Tip Sheet: Narrative Voice

I. WORDS

What kind of vocabulary does the author favor? Does she use long words or short ones, Anglo-Saxon words or Latinate words, colorful words or plain ones, an expansive vocabulary or a limited one, lots of slang and jargon or very little?

Does the author rely more on verbs and nouns, or on adverbs and adjectives?

Does the author choose words for their literal meaning, or for their color, sound, emotional weight, and subtle connotations?

2. SENTENCES AND PARAGRAPHS

Does the author favor short or long sentences? Short or long paragraphs?

Are the sentences constructed simply (subject—verb—object) or are they more complex (including compound sentences, subordinate clauses, etc.)?

How much variety is there in the structure of sentences and paragraphs?

Does the author's approach to sentences and paragraphs vary according to the type and purpose of the scene, or is it consistent throughout the story?

3. RHYTHM

What kind of rhythm does the prose have when it is read aloud?

How much does the author vary the rhythm for different kinds of characters, events, or scenes?

4. DEGREE OF FORMALITY

Is the tone of the story casual and informal or formal and proper?

Does the author adhere to proper grammar or take liberties with it?

5. LINEAR VERSUS LAYERED NARRATIVE

Is the narrative straightforward, linear, and presented in chronological order? Or is it layered, elliptical, branching, or pieced together like a quilt?

To what extent does the author move about from present to past or future events?

What devices does the author use to move around in time (e.g., frames or flashbacks)?

6. BALANCE AMONG ACTION, DIALOGUE, DESCRIPTION, AND EXPOSITION

What is the blend or balance of action, dialogue, and description? How much of each does the author use? Which does he favor?

To what extent does the author show, not tell? Does the author impart information through scenes or through exposition?

How much of the story is focused internally (i.e., the thoughts or interior life of a character) and how much is focused externally (i.e., on action, or on observations of the character from outside)?

7. DETAILS

What kinds of details does the author use to describe a person, event, or scene?

Is the author lavish or sparing in the use of details? Is the style lush or lean?

How does the author direct the reader's attention? What does she hold up for the reader to notice?

8. SUSPENSE

What level of suspense does the story strive for?

What techniques, either of plot or of language, does the author use to create or heighten the suspense?

9. PACE

Does the story move quickly or at a leisurely rate?

Does the pace vary from scene to scene, according to what the scene is about?

10. HUMOR

How much humor is blended into the story?

What kind of humor is it?

11. EMOTIONAL COLOR

Does the author bring a lot of emotion into the prose, or does he present "just the facts"?

12. REGIONALISM, CULTURAL FLAVOR

To what extent does the author incorporate the speech patterns, expressions, attitudes, and beliefs of a particular region or culture into the narrative?

13. IMAGERY, METAPHOR, AND SIMILE

How much or how little does the author use images, metaphors, and similes to create an impression or an effect?

Is there a particular arena from which these images tend to be drawn (e.g., nature, food, wars and battles)?

14. SYMBOLS

How much or how little does the author use symbols to highlight a theme or create an effect?

How obvious or subtle is the symbolism?

15. ALLUSIONS AND REFERENCES

What kinds of allusions or references does the author make or have the characters make? Famous poems? Bible stories or classical myths? Renaissance paintings, Impressionism, modern art? Classical music, jazz, rap, rock? Sports? Brand names of products? The military? Politics? TV or film?

To what extent does the author use such illusions or references?

16. WORLDVIEW

Does the author share with the reader a distinctive attitude, perspective, or worldview?

Does the main character have a distinctive attitude, perspective, or worldview?

Does the author seem to be familiar with the milieu of the story and to have a point of view about it?

Does the story seem to reflect the background, experiences, memories, and passions of the author and the main character?

17. CONSISTENCY

Is the voice consistent throughout the story?

Does the reader come away with an underlying sense that the author is in control of what she is writing?

Exercises: Discovering and Developing Your Voice

1. Choose three short stories by different authors to read and think about. For each story write brief answers to the following questions:

   a. Which three of the seventeen qualities of narrative voice contributed most to the way the author told the story?

   b. Which three of the qualities of narrative voice contributed least?

   c. Considering the three authors together, which one do you think had a particularly strong, effective, or interesting voice? Why?

2. The paragraph below *tells* us about Larry and his dilemma. Write a scene or a sequence of scenes that reveals the same information by *showing* it.

> Larry had lived in Midvale all his forty years, which he felt was about thirty-nine years too many. But he was stuck. His wife Barbara liked being so close to her sister and her parents, especially now that her mother was sick. The kids—Jonathan, age nine, and Kim, age thirteen with all its accompanying annoyances—were settled into their schools and their activities with friends. Larry was doing well at the bank, even though the work bored him stiff, and he didn't dare quit, not with the mortgage on the fancy new house staring him in the face. Barbara called the place her dream palace, although frankly Larry preferred their old home on Maplewood Drive. Life would be forty more years of the same dreary stuff, Larry figured—unless he could figure out a way to implement his Secret Plan.

3. Select a story you have written or a scene you wrote for an exercise in this book (Larry's scene or one from an earlier chapter). Identify which three of the seventeen qualities of voice you think you emphasized most in the writing of it. Write a paragraph describing the following:

■ How each of the three qualities contributes to your voice in the story. (Use the questions in the Tip Sheet: Narrative Voice as a guide.)

■ Why you approached each quality in the particular way that you did.

4. Write two new scenes based on the one you described in Exercise 3. (If you chose a story for that exercise, select a typical scene from it for this exercise.)

Scene 1: Concentrate on the same three qualities of voice, but approach them in a different manner (e.g., if you choose words as one of the three qualities you are working with, use a different kind of vocabulary).

Scene 2: Focus on three new qualities of voice to see the different effects that changing the voice can help you achieve.

5. From the lists below, choose two characters, a setting, and a situation. Write two scenes in which the people are in this place discussing this problem or circumstance. Think about how you can use various qualities of voice to create the effect you want.

Scene 1: Make the pace fast and the mood tense. Concentrate on action and dialogue—keep description and exposition to a minimum. Assume that the characters are eager to resolve the matter at hand.

Scene 2: Make the pace slower and the mood dreamy and relaxed. Add description and a little exposition to the mix of action and dialog. Assume that at least one of the characters is trying to avoid a discussion of the matter at hand.

Characters:

A rebellious teenager.

A university student on the verge of flunking out.

Someone who has been passed over for a promotion at work.

An itinerant carpenter.

A professional thief.

Someone who married for money and is unhappy with his or her spouse.

Someone with a new job who feels out of his or her depth.

A visitor from another planet who is disguised as a human.

A middle-aged person who finds his or her life boring.

Someone whose work has been recognized with a substantial award or prize.

A pregnant woman whose child is due any day.

An adult who has never forgiven his or her parents for perceived wrongs.

Someone who recently quit a corporate job to take up a career in acting.

The neighborhood busybody.

Someone who feels it is his or her mission to do good for humankind.

Settings:

At a stable that boards horses.

In the posh head office of a prosperous corporation.

In the back room of a hardware store.

In a cheap hotel room in Paris.

In the stands at a college football game.

In the cocktail lounge of a luxury hotel.

In a Las Vegas or Atlantic City casino.

In a cabana at a Hawaiian beach resort.

At a truckstop lunch counter along the interstate highway.

On a crowded subway train at the commute hour.

In the backstage area of a college or community theater.

On an airliner during a cross-country flight.

Waiting in line to see Pirates of the Caribbean at Disneyland.

On a hiking trail to a waterfall at Yosemite.

Outside a church on Sunday morning.

Situations:

Character A has discovered an embarrassing secret about Character B.

The two characters encounter each other for the first time in many years.

Character A becomes convinced he or she has seen a ghost.

Bad weather has forced the cancellation of a long-planned and happily anticipated event.

A valuable piece of jewelry has disappeared.

One of the characters arrived home to find something seriously amiss.

One of the characters has been caught sneaking around someplace where he or she doesn't belong.

One of the characters has just learned that he or she will be moving to a new home in a distant place.

Character A has caught Character B lying about a matter of great importance.

Character A is asking Character B to help him or her out of a serious jam. Providing help would require doing something illegal, immoral, or unethical.

Character A has just met Mr. or Ms. Right. Character B believes the new lover is really Mr. or Ms. Wrong.

The characters have just had a huge fight. Both regret it, but neither is willing to admit being wrong.

Character A has just won a $1 million lottery jackpot. Unbeknownst to Character A, Character B is about to file for bankruptcy.

An investment scheme has turned out to be a fraud, and the investors have lost everything. Character A had talked Character B into investing his or her life savings in the scheme.

One of the characters is planning to run away from home.

Suggested Reading

Exploring the Realm of Short Stories

The best way to learn about short stories and how they work is to read them—read lots of them, sampling a wide variety of authors and genres and styles. Every short story you read will help you understand the essential ingredients of fiction and the effective techniques for handling them.

To help you embark on this literary adventure, some possibilities for reading are listed here. These stories, by no means a definitive or comprehensive list, were chosen for the skillful or interesting way they present one of the five ingredients—characters, conflict, structure, setting, or narrative voice. Of course, during the writing process these elements blend together and influence each other, making it difficult to pull them apart once the story is completed. You can read any short story with an eye to any of the five categories. Each story in the Plot and Structure list, for example, can also be examined instructively for the way the author has handled the characters, conflict, setting, or narrative voice.

The list spans more than a century of writing and includes stories that are considered classics by acknowledged masters as well as new works by younger writers still making their mark. All the stories can be found in anthologies or collections at your bookstore or library. Ready for more reading? One good way to find inspiration and trace trends in the short story form is to seek out two series of anthologies that produce annual volumes: *The Best American Short Stories* and *Prize Stories of the O. Henry*

Memorial Awards. The editors collect what they consider to be the finest short stories that appeared in magazines and literary journals in the U.S. and Canada during the preceding year. Both series have been publishing for about eighty years.

CHARACTERS

Alison Baker, *Better Be Ready 'Bout Half Past Eight*
Maeve Binchy, *The Lilac Bus*
John Cheever, *The Five-Forty-Eight*
Sir Arthur Conan Doyle, *A Scandal in Bohemia*
William Faulkner, *A Rose for Emily*
Tess Gallagher, *The Lover of Horses*
Ellen Gilchrist, *Revenge*
Ring Lardner, *Haircut*
James Thurber, *The Secret Life of Walter Mitty*
Chelsea Quinn Yarbro, *Variations on a Theme*

CONFLICT

Stephen Vincent Benét, *The Devil and Daniel Webster*
Charles Dickens, *A Christmas Carol*
Jack London, *To Build a Fire*
Margaret Lucke, *Identity Crisis*
Bharati Mukherjee, *The Management of Grief*
Cynthia Ozick, *The Shawl*
Amy Tan, *Two Kinds*
P.G. Wodehouse, *Jeeves Takes Charge*

PLOTTING AND STRUCTURE

Donald Barthelme, *The School*
Lawrence Block, *Some Days You Get the Bear*
Janet Dawson, *Little Red Corvette*
Stanley Elkin, *A Poetics for Bullies*
Charlotte Perkins Gilman, *The Yellow Wallpaper*
Shirley Jackson, *The Lottery*
Alice Munro, *Miles City, Montana*
Tim O'Brien, *The Things They Carried*

SETTING AND ATMOSPHERE

Ray Bradbury, *There Will Come Soft Rains*
Susan Dunlap, *Death and Diamonds*
William Gass, *In the Heart of the Heart of the Country*
Lorrie Moore, *Terrific Mother*
Maxine O'Callaghan, *Wolf Winter*
John Updike, *The Persistence of Desire*
Eudora Welty, *Death of a Traveling Salesman*
Tobias Wolff, *Hunters in the Snow*

NARRATIVE VOICE

James Baldwin, *Sonny's Blues*
Toni Cade Bambera, *Gorilla, My Love*
Raymond Carver, *Are These Actual Miles?*
Louise Erdrich, *Fleur*
Ernest Hemingway, *A Clean, Well-Lighted Place*
David Leavitt, *Gravity*
Ursula K. Le Guin, *The Ones Who Walk Away from Omelas*
Mary Morris, *The Bus of Dreams*

When Your Story Is Written

A Quick Guide to Submitting Manuscripts for Publication

Q.: I've written a short story that I think is pretty good, although it might benefit from a little more work. But I'm so close to it, I can't really judge what it needs. How can I find out?

A.: Let someone read it who will give you thoughtful, honest, and supportive criticism. All three elements are vital. You want a reader who is willing to point out both flaws and virtues and who is discerning enough to be able to explain why she feels an element in your story does or doesn't work, and in the latter case, to suggest how it might be remedied. Moreover, you want someone who can do this in a way that doesn't dishearten you but encourages you to keep writing.

If your best friend or significant other fills this bill, that's great; but frequently this isn't the case. Someone who's close to you may find it hard to be objective. A better choice might be another writer or a group of your fellow scribes.

Q.: Sounds good. But where do I find other writers?

A.: Here are some suggestions:

- *Attend a writers' conference. One-day, weekend, and longer conferences for writers abound. They are sponsored by colleges, bookstores, and writers' organizations. Not only do they provide an enjoyable opportunity to focus intensely on your*

147

writing, many of them invite you to submit a story manuscript for evaluation by one of the participating faculty.

■ **Enroll in a fiction writing workshop.** *Check out possibilities offered by community colleges, adult education programs, university extension programs, city recreation departments, and local bookstores. Some workshops are open to both adults and teens. Find out about the format of the class or workshop you are considering. Look for one in which students are encouraged to read their works in progress to the group to obtain feedback from other participants.*

■ **Go on-line.** *The Internet offers a wealth of possibilities for communicating and sharing work with other writers.*

■ **Join a writers' organization.** *A number of national organizations exist to help writers, and some of them have active local chapters that welcome new members.*

■ **Form your own critique group.** *Gather four to six writers who will commit to meeting once or twice a month to read and comment on each other's work. Where do you find them? Through the connections you make at conferences, workshops, and organizational meetings.*

Workshops and critique groups are particularly valuable for four reasons:

1. *You will enjoy the fellowship and support of others who understand from experience the struggles and joys of writing.*

2. *You will receive valuable feedback on your work. Listen to everyone's opinion, but remember, it's your story. Half the comments you get may be off the mark, and you're free to ignore them. The other fifty percent may prove invaluable.*

3. *You will learn to identify strengths and weaknesses in other people's stories, and to bring that newly honed critical sharpness to your own work.*

4. *You'll have an incentive to sit down and write. You won't want to show up at too many meetings without having a few fresh pages in hand.*

Q.: How can I tell when my story is as good as I can make it?

A.: *That's something only you can decide. Chances are it will never be perfect, and that's fine, because there is no such thing as perfect in literature. If you cling to your story too closely, if you rework it too often, you can rob it of its freshness and vitality.*

If you've done your best with the story, have someone read it whose judgment you value and trust. Then decide if it will benefit substantially from more of your time and attention. Chances are good that at this point it's time to send this story out into the world to seek its fortune, and to turn your energy to writing a new one.

Q.: How do I decide where to send my story?

A.: *By doing some market research. There are two principal types of markets for short stories—magazines and anthologies. Although magazines print fewer short stories than they used to, they still provide the most plentiful opportunities for publication, especially the literary journals and those devoted to specific genres such as mystery, horror, or science fiction. Most anthologies reprint stories that have appeared previously in magazines or solicit contributions from authors known to the editors, but some accept submissions of original stories from new writers.*

To seek out the markets most likely to be receptive to your work, check your library or bookstore for magazines that publish similar types of stories. Several periodicals for writers, such as Writer's Digest, The Writer, Poets & Writers, *and the offbeat* Gila Queen's Guide to Markets, *regularly include market listings for magazines and anthologies.* Writer's Digest Books *publishes an annual directory called* Writer's Market *as well as the biannual* Fiction Writer's Market. *(Their addresses are listed at the end of this section.)*

When you have identified several prospective markets, send for copies of their writers' guidelines. Most publications will provide them gladly if you include a self-addressed, stamped envelope. For a small cost, you can obtain sample copies. It's a good idea to read an issue or two to make sure your story and the publication are a good fit. Editors are not impressed when they receive stories that, no matter how beautifully written, are completely unsuitable for their magazines.

Q.: I've found a market that seems like just the right home for my story. How do I go about submitting it?

A.: *First, make sure your presentation is polished and professional. Follow the guidelines in Appendix C, How to Format Your Manuscript. Double-check it one more time to make sure that all the spelling is correct and no typographical errors have crept in.*

Some editors like you to include a cover letter; others don't think it is important. The writers' guidelines or market listings usually indicate the magazine's preference. If you decide to include a letter, make it brief and businesslike. Say that you are submitting your story, titled "Story Name," for the editor's consideration and express thanks for his or her time and attention. If you have some relevant publishing credits, mention them. If you don't, then don't bring the matter up. Leave out any comments about the quality of the prose, the reasons why the editor should buy the story, or your trials and tribulations as a writer. Let the story speak for itself.

Mail your manuscript flat in a nine- by twelve-inch envelope, and include a self-addressed, stamped envelope for the editor's reply. Make sure the postage you provide is sufficient for the manuscript's return in the event that the editor is not sensible enough to buy it. You can also tell the editor that it's not necessary to return the manuscript and simply include an envelope with a first-class stamp for a letter reply.

Q.: How long should I wait for a reply?

A.: *The publication's writers' guidelines often indicate the typical turnaround time. If they don't, give the editor at least a couple of months. Many smaller journals are run by small staffs who have a huge number of submissions to deal with. If three months go by without a response, gently nudge the editor with a polite phone call or note.*

Q.: Can I submit my story to more than one market at a time?

A.: Traditionally, simultaneous submissions were frowned upon. Now fewer journals object, but most prefer to be told that you are not giving them an exclusive look at your story.

Q.: **What about copyright and other rights?**

A.: Most magazines are copyrighted, and your copyright is in force under theirs. Usually what you are selling to a magazine is the first American serial rights—that is, the journal has the right to publish the story one time, and to be the first periodical in the United States to do so. The rights for any subsequent publication—in a book, for example—remain yours. Occasionally an editor will ask to purchase all rights to your short story. It is in your best interest to say no and hold on to your rights, even if it means forfeiting an opportunity to be published.

Some writers like to specify on the manuscript what rights they are offering. If you want to include this information, place it in the upper right corner of the first page, above the word count.

Q.: **Suppose my story is accepted. What can I expect to be paid?**

A.: In that happy event, call all your friends and celebrate. It's truly a moment to savor.

Don't expect to be become rich, though. Although a few markets pay well, many prestigious journals operate on tight budgets and can only offer a few pennies or even a fraction of a cent per word. Some provide payment in the form of free copies of the magazine.

Q.: **What happens if my story is turned down?**

A.: Welcome to the club. Rejection happens sooner or later to every writer. I was once greatly cheered to read in a biography of F. Scott Fitzgerald that this acclaimed author collected nearly three hundred rejection slips before he sold a story.

Many writers set publication as their ultimate goal. Being published, they believe, is the stamp of success—an acknowledgement of their story's excellence and a validation of their worth as writers. Certainly it is exciting and gratifying to see your name in print.

But the fact is, the short story market is tight. Many highly accomplished stories are turned down. A rejection is not a comment on your talent or on the merits of your work. It simply means that one editor, for one publication, on one particular day, chose not to buy your story. Possibly the editor bought a similar story the previous week. Perhaps the magazine was overstocked; most receive hundreds more submissions than they can possibly print.

Your next step is to put your story into a fresh envelope and send it to the next market on your list. Then get busy writing your next story.

The key to getting published is to persevere. It has been said that if you must choose between talent and persistence, you should pick persistence. A talented writer who gives up won't succeed. A less-gifted one who perseveres probably will. So write. Write some more. Keep on writing. Put your stories in the mail instead of in your desk drawer, and look forward to the day when you receive a letter from an editor that begins, "We are pleased to inform you...."

ADDRESSES FOR INFORMATION SOURCES

Writer's Digest and Writer's Digest Books, 1507 Dana Avenue, Cincinnati, OH 45207

The Writer, 120 Boylston Street, Boston, MA 02116

Poets & Writers, 72 Spring Street, New York, NY 10012

The Gila Queen's Guide to Markets, PO Box 97, Newton, NJ 07860

J. Q. Author
123 Literary Street
Storyville, CA 94199
(212) 555-6789

APPENDIX C
HOW TO FORMAT YOUR MANUSCRIPT
by J. Q. Author

These instructions show how editors and publishers expect your manuscript to look when you submit a short story for publication.

Center the title about halfway down the page. Beneath it, center your byline, either your real name or a pseudonym, as you want it to appear when published. Your real name goes in the upper left corner, along with your contact information. Put an approximate word count in the upper right corner.

Always type or word process your story. The word "manuscript" comes from the Latin *manu* (hand) and *scriptus* (written), but handwritten manuscripts are unacceptable. So are fancy fonts with ruffles and flourishes. Straightforward serif fonts, like this one or this one are the most reader friendly. Serifs are the little feet at the tops and bottoms of the letters. This font is sans serif—*sans* is French for without.

Use standard white paper, 8 1/2 x 11 inches, typing on only one side of the page. Twenty-pound bond is fine; that's the paper typically used in laser printers and photocopiers. Make the type black, crisp, and clear; in other words, clean the keys if you're using a typewriter, and avoid dot matrix mode on computer printers.

Double space the text. Indent the paragraphs one-half inch, and don't skip a space between paragraphs. In their writers' guidelines, publishers often ask writers not to justify the text (making all the lines exactly the same length) but to leave the right margin ragged, as shown here. On some printers, justified margins result in awkward word or letter spacing that can make the manuscript hard to read.

Speaking of margins, leave at least a one-inch margin all around.

On the second and subsequent pages, put a slug line at the top with your name, key words from the title, and the page number, as shown above.

When you reach the end of your story, say so as shown below. That way the editor can be sure there are no pages missing.

Before you send out your manuscript, double check it. Is all the spelling and grammar correct? Have any words or sentences been scrambled or dropped? Don't trust your spellchecker to do the job for you; it'll let the sentence *Male thee Czech two hymn* slide through just fine.

It's SOP (standard operating procedure) to enclose an SASE (self-addressed, stamped envelope) for the editor's reply.

Good luck!

—End—

Index

Active words, using, 126-127
Adjectives and adverbs, sparing use of, 45, 127
Answer, direction, of plot towards, 72, 78-79
Art of Dramatic Writing, The, 31
Atmosphere of story, 11, 99-119 (*see also* Setting)
Atwood, Margaret, 9

Back story, 31-32
Ballad of Lucy Whipple, The, 8
Beginning of story, 85-87
Believability of character's actions, 33-38
Best American Short Stories, The, 143-144
Binchy, Maeve, 75, 144
Bio chart for character, 41
Blind Men and the Elephant, The, 75
Bradbury, Ray, 100, 145

Causality and connectedness of events in plot, 72, 76-78
Characters, creating, 11, 21-53, 144
 in conflict, 72-73
 dialogue as voice of, 42-50
  attributions, 45-46
  body language, 48
  functions, 42
  paragraph, new, for each speaker, 48

readers, incorporating, 44-48
stage business, using effectively, 46-48
"suggestive" dialogue, 44-45
tip sheet, 44, 49-50
voice for each, 43-44
exercises, 51-53
as first essential ingredient, 21
life for characters, 29-38
 back story, 31-32
 believability of actions, 33-38
 bio chart, 41
 with emotions and contradictions, 32-33
 with past and future, 31-32
 three-dimensional, 30-31, 39-40
point of view, choosing, 22-23
 protagonist, choosing, 22-23
 readings, suggested, 144
Cheever, John, 22, 144
Christmas Carol, A, 79, 144
Climax of plot, 81
Closure, 4, 79
Complications in plot, 80
Conflict, 11
 readings, suggested, 144
Contradictions of characters, 32-33
Copyrights, 151
Crisis in plot, 80
Critique groups, value of, 148
Cushman, Karen, 8

Dawson, Jant 76-77, 144
Death of a Traveling Salesmen, 100
Deluxe Transvestite Vampire, The, 125-126
Denouement of plot, 81
Deus ex machina, 77-78
Dialogue, creating, as voice of character, 42-50 (*see also* Characters, creating)
Dickens, Charles, 79, 144
Domino theory, of plotting, 76-77
Drafts, using three, 16-17
  importance of, 130
Dreaming of Dragons, 24, 92
Dunlap, Susan, 101, 145

Egri, Lajos, 31
Elements of Style, The, 125
Emotions of characters, 32-33
End of story, 90-92
Exciting force of plot, 80

Faulkner, William, 24, 74, 144
Fiction Writer's Market, 149, 152
Five-Forty-Eight, The, 22, 144
Flashbacks, 74, 132
Frames, 74

Gila Queen's Guide to Markets, The, 149, 152
Goal of story, 3-4
Gordon, Karen Elizabeth, 125
Guide to submitting manuscript for publication, 147-152

Handmade's Tale, The, 9
High concept, 70
The Hitchhiker, 59
Hunters in the Snow, 124

Ideas for story, finding, 5-10 (*see also* Starting story)
Identity Crisis, 7
Imitation, avoiding, 132-133
Inciting incident of plot, 80
Information, four ways to give, 131

Ingredients of story, four basic, 10-12 (*see also* Starting)

Language, understanding, fundamentals of, 125-126
  power of, 132
Length of story, 5
Lilac Bus, The, 75, 144
London, Jack, 62-63, 144
Lucke, Margaret, 144

Management of Grief, The, 60, 100, 144
Manuscript, guide to submitting for publication, 147-152
  formatting, 153-154
Menkin, Larry, 18
Middle of story, 87-90
Movement of plot forward in time, 72, 73-76
Mukherjee, Bharati, 60, 100, 144

Narrative structure, building, 79-83 (*see also* Plot and structure of story)
Narrative voice, 12, 121-141, 145
  as "artful way" story is told, 122
  exercises, 138-141
  personalizing, 132-133
  protagonist, most significant factor in choice of, 124
  qualities of, 122-123, 134-137
  readings, suggested, 145
  strength of, increasing, 124-132
    active verbs, using, 126-127
    adjectives and adverbs, sparing use of, 127
    language of, understanding fundamentals of, 125-126
    language, understanding fundamentals of, 125-126
    language, power of, 132
    passive voice, avoiding, 128
    waffle words, care with, 127
    words as basic tool, 126-132
  tip sheet, 123, 134-137
  what it is, 122-124
New Well-Tempered Sentence, The, 125-126
No Wildflower, 25

O'Brien, Tim, 94, 144
Old Furiosity Shoppe, The, 86-87
Ozick, Cynthia, 62, 144

Passive voice, avoiding, 128
Perseverance, 152
Planning story, 70-72
Playing for Keeps, 112
Plot and structure of story, 11, 69-97, 144
  beginning, 85-87
  characteristics, four, 72-79
    answer or resolution, direction toward, 72, 78-79
    causality and connectedness of events, 72, 76-78
    character in conflict, 72-73
    deus ex machina, 77-78
    domino theory of plotting, 76-77
    flashbacks, 74
    frames, 74
    movement, forward in time, 72, 73-76
  end, 90-92
  exercises, 96-97
  middle, 87-90
  narrative structure, building, 79-83
    Cinderella, analogy to, 81-83
    climax, 81
    complications, 80
    crisis, 80
    denouement, 81
    inciting incident, 80
  as organizational system, 69
  readings, suggested, 144
  scenes, 92-94
  stories without, 94-95
  what it is, 69-72
    definition, 70
    plans, 70-72
    versus premise, 70
Plot point, 80
Poets & Writers, 149, 152
Point of view, chossing, 23-28, (*see also* Characters)
Premise versus plot, 70
Prize Stories of the O. Henry Memorial Awards, 143-144
Protagonist, choosing, 22-23

Quinn, Yarbro, Chelsea, 23, 63, 111, 144

Readers, inviting in, techniques for, 111-114
Readings, suggested, 143-145
  Best American Short Stories, The, 143-144
  characters, 144
  conflict, 144
  narrative voice, 145
  plotting and structure, 144
  Prize Stories of the O. Henry Memorial Awards, 143-144
  setting and atmosphere, 145
Rejection, 151-152
Relative Stranger, A, 30
Resolution, 4
  direction of plot toward, 72, 78-79
Rose for Emily, A, 24, 74, 144
Rules, absence of, 12-13

Saxe, John Godfrey, 75
Scenes, 92-94
Setting and atmoshpere of story, 11, 99-119, 145
  bringing it to life, 107-114
    readers, inviting in, 111-114
    three dimensions, 108-110, 115-117
    time as fourth dimension, 110-111
  choosing, 101-107
    actual place, fictionalizing, 105-107
    imaginary, 107
    people and place, interaction of, 102-105
    "what if..." game, 101
  exercises, 118-119
  readings, suggested, 145
  tip sheet, 109, 115-117
Shawl, The, 62, 144
Starting story, 1-20
  advantages of short story form, 2
  closure, 4
  definitions, 2
  drafts, three, purpose of, 16-17
  exercises, 19-20
  fiction vs. reality, 3
  goal, 3-4
  ideas, 5-10

Starting story (*cont.*)
    active search for, 7-8
    flour analogy, 6-7
    sources, 7-8
    synergy of two/more ideas, 8-9
    "thinking story," 9-10
    "what if..." game, 9-10
    ingredients, four basic, 10-12
        characters, 11
        conflict, 11
        plot and structure, 11-12
        setting, 12
    length, 5
    narrative voice, 12
    process of writing, 12-18
    reasons for writing, two, 1
    resolution, 4
    rules, absence of, 12-13
    theme, 4-5
    voice, 12
Structure of story, 11
    building, 70-83 (*see also* Plot)
Strunk, William, Jr., 125

Tan, Amy, 61, 144
Theme of story, 4-5
There Will Come Soft Rains, 100, 145
Things They Carried, The, 94-95
Thinking story, 9-10
Third person narrative, 25-28

    limited omniscient, 27-28
    limited or restricted, 26
    multiple, 26
    omniscient, 26-27
Time, using as fourth dimension, 110-111
To Build a Fire, 62-63, 144
Two Kinds, 61, 144

Variations on a Theme, 23, 144
Voice of story, 12, 121-141 (*see also* Narrative)

Waffle words, care in using, 127
Welty, Eudora, 100, 145
"What if..." game, 9-10, 78, 90, 101
White E. B., 125
Witness, 83
Wolff, Tobias, 124, 145
Words as basic tool, 126-132 (*see also* Narrative)
Workshops, value of, 148
Writer, The, 149, 152
Writer's Digest, 149, 152
Writers, other, how to find, 147-148, 152
Writing:
    as mode of exploration, 1
    process, 12-18
    rules for, absence of, 12-13

Margaret Lucke

Margaret Lucke is the author of the novel *A Relative Stranger* (St. Martin's Press), which was nominated for an Anthony Award for Best First Mystery Novel, and coauthor of the children's adventure *Who Stole Travada?* (Adventure Press). Her short stories have appeared in anthologies and on the *Salon* literary magazine site on the World Wide Web.

She has taught fiction writing classes for University of California, Berkeley, Extension since 1994 and conducts writing workshops for elementary schools, libraries, and teachers groups. As an editorial consultant of fiction writers, she has helped numerous individuals to reach their writing goals.

Ms. Lucke's other publications include more than 50 newspaper and magazine features and the how-to book *Outdoor Storage* (Ortho Books). She also produces marketing and management materials for businesses and organizations.

CPSIA information can be obtained
at www.ICGtesting.com
Printed in the USA
BVHW080331260921
617559BV00004B/16

9 780070 390775